BY SWERVE OF SHORE
Exploring Dublin's Coast

By the same author

The Wicklow Way
By Cliff and Shore
Irish Long Distance Walks
Ireland's Way Marked Trails
Ireland's Waterside Walks

BY SWERVE
OF
SHORE

Exploring Dublin's Coast

Michael Fewer

GILL & MACMILLAN

Gill & Macmillan Ltd
Goldenbridge
Dublin 8
with associated companies throughout the world
© Michael Fewer 1998
0 7171 2718 4
Illustrations by Michael Fewer
Index compiled by Helen Litton
Design and print origination by
O'K Graphic Design, Dublin

This book is typeset in Adobe Garamond 10/14 pt.

A catalogue record for this book is available from the British Library.

1 3 5 4 2

For Teresa

'. . . from swerve of shore
to bend of bay . . . '

James Joyce, *Finnegans Wake*

Contents

Prologue

When I was a small boy the vastness and power of the ocean impressed me greatly. I delighted particularly in the tidal zone, a littoral wonderland teeming with colourful and strange life forms, and I whiled away many summer hours collecting them with shrimp net and bucket. As I grew older, I began to take notice of wider aspects of the seashore, such as the lighthouses and the harbours, and how the very skeleton of the land was exposed to view in layers along the sea cliffs. It was clear that the coast was an enormously rich habitat, for, despite the sometimes harsh conditions, many more species of flora and fauna thrived along the shore than further inland or further out to sea.

My fascination and interest have grown over the years, and not long ago I indulged my passion for the coast by completing a long-dreamed of odyssey when I explored, on foot, the County Waterford coast from Youghal Bridge to Waterford Harbour. I recorded my experiences in words and drawings, later published in a book called *By Cliff and Shore*, and found the experience so enjoyable that when my wife Teresa suggested that I research a similar book on the coast of County Dublin, I warmed to the idea immediately. Dublin's coast, after all, is very rich in its history, topographically diverse, a mixture of urban and rural landscapes, and it is easily accessible.

I knew that much of the Dublin coast would be visible from the summit of Three Rock Mountain, so I climbed it early one spring morning and was delighted to find that not only could I clearly see the shore to beyond Skerries, identified by its offshore islands, but that the Carlingford peninsula, with its backdrop of the Mournes, was also sharply defined. From that vantage-point,

I could trace the Dublin coast southwards to the hill of Howth, from where it took a broad sweep to the west to form Dublin Bay. Only the last couple of miles of shore were hidden from my view behind Killiney Hill. The projected walk seemed quite short, but a later examination of the maps brought to my notice something that was not fully clear from the mountain top. As the crow flies, County Dublin stretches thirty miles north to south. Besides the great bight of Dublin Bay, however, the seashore meanders inland in three places to the north of Howth, at Baldoyle, Malahide and Rogerstown, the last two extending nearly four miles to the west. These extensive narrow-entranced tidal inlets, protected from the open sea by substantial sandbars, add to the variety of the coastscape, and would increase the length of my journey.

The project was becoming more inviting, but I wondered just how much of the coast it would be possible to walk along without being deflected inland by private property reaching down to the shore. (I had completed all but three of Waterford's one hundred and twenty-five miles of coast before I had the embarrassment of being ordered out of someone's back garden!) There was only one way to find out: I had to try it. Brendan Grimes, a friend who lives in Skerries, assured me that he had walked many miles of the coast and said that he would accompany me on a 'sample' trek, the first few miles of the Dublin shore from the Meath border south to his home. I was delighted to take up his suggestion, and we arranged to do it on an April day.

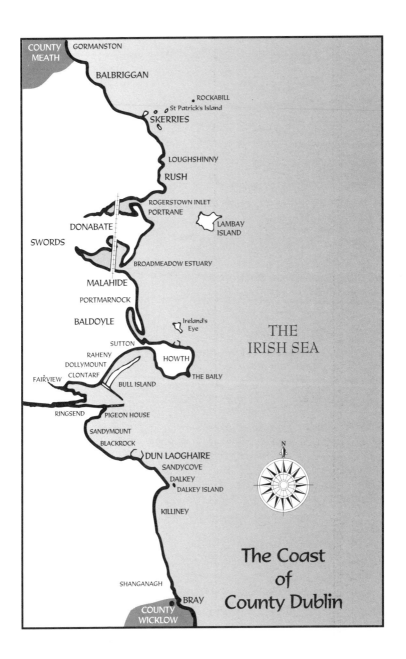

COUNTY MEATH

GORMANSTON

BALBRIGGAN

ROCKABILL

St Patrick's Island

SKERRIES

LOUGHSHINNY

RUSH

ROGERSTOWN INLET

PORTRANE

DONABATE

LAMBAY ISLAND

SWORDS

BROADMEADOW ESTUARY

MALAHIDE

PORTMARNOCK

BALDOYLE

Ireland's Eye

SUTTON

RAHENY

DOLLYMOUNT

FAIRVIEW CLONTARF

HOWTH

THE BAILY

BULL ISLAND

THE IRISH SEA

RINGSEND PIGEON HOUSE

SANDYMOUNT

BLACKROCK

DUN LAOGHAIRE

SANDYCOVE

DALKEY

DALKEY ISLAND

KILLINEY

N

The Coast of County Dublin

SHANGANAGH

BRAY

COUNTY WICKLOW

1

South to Skerries

At the southern extremity of Royal Meath's six-mile coastline the swift-flowing Delvin river enters the Irish Sea. On the broad beach beside the river where it meets the sea, St Patrick is said to have baptised a local chieftain and a great gathering of his clan. The chieftain's son, Benen, was so inspired by Patrick that, when the evangelist continued southwards on his mission, Benen accompanied him. In time, the young man's scholarly ability and his new-found love of Christ took him into the priesthood and he went on to found churches in Galway and the Aran Islands. On the death of Patrick, it was Benen, as Benignus, who took over as his successor as archbishop of Armagh. At this place, where the waters of the Delvin river enter the Irish Sea, with no one about but myself, Brendan and his dog, I began my exploration of the County Dublin coastline.

On the basis of this six-mile stretch along the shore southwards to the town of Skerries, I would decide whether or not to walk the rest of the coast to the border of County Wicklow, just short of the town of Bray, about thirty miles to the south as the crow flies, but, following the coastline, at least seventy-five miles away.

Brendan had brought along his dog, a young black Labrador called Megan, which he was training. His wife Olivia had driven us by car from Skerries and dropped us at the shore on the Meath side of the river. To the north, a broad beach stretched for miles towards where the Mourne mountains formed a pale blue backdrop to the hills of the Cooley Peninsula. To the south, the long beach came to an end against a field of ragged, black volcanic rock. I had picked a good day to start — a bright, blue-skied April day; the air was filled with lark song, backed by the muted hiss of the waves on the shore.

I had thought that such a small river, which hardly featured on the map, would be crossed easily, but our first surprise of the day was the depth and speed of the waters, which ruled out any stepping-stone crossing. Flexibility and the frequent need to make quick changes of plan are some of the characteristics of coast-walking, however, and the lattice steel bridge, which carries the main Dublin to Belfast railway across the river, offered an alternative, if possibly illegal, solution to the problem.

Within minutes we had climbed the railway embankment, and after waiting for an Inter-City train to go whooshing by, we set out across the utilitarian timber plank surface of the bridge, thirty feet above the Delvin, which glinted through great gaps between the boards. Megan refused to move out along the planks, so Brendan had to pick her up and carry her across in his arms. In this way we came to the southern bank of the Delvin, where the coast of County Dublin begins.

We followed a stony shore that was strewn with razor-shells, large cockles and clams. After crossing a rocky outcrop that reached out into the sea, we came to a tiny and idyllic crescent of sand. Just inland of this were the ruins of a building, partially surrounded by a high wall. We made our way to it and pottered about an overgrown courtyard, puzzling over the high walls, curious circular windows, and the stunted remains of a few exotic conifers. Megan, sensing our curiosity, redoubled the excited sniffing she had been at since we started, sticking her nose into clumps of nettles without seeming to be harmed, and darting to and fro, tail a-wag. Nature had so well re-established itself that it was difficult in places to guess where the house ended and where the walled garden began. Great rounded clumps of arching, thick brambles hid the base of the walls; trunks of ash and elder exuded from the crumbling masonry to reach skywards, and clusters of valerian were spreading destructive roots through the lime-rich tops of what remained of the walls.

It was clear that the building had been sited just inland of the tiny sandy cove, the only such cove among the expanses of rough, volcanic bedrock that extended southwards from the outlet of the Delvin. As we moved away from the ruin and continued along the shore, we saw ahead the crouched figure of a man in the midst of the dark Silurian outcrops. Bucket in hand, he was carefully harvesting some crop from the gleaming wet rocks left exposed by the dropping tide.

'He might know something about that place,' Brendan said, and we made our way over to him through a maze of rock pools.

He was an elderly but robust, balding man in wellington boots and was picking periwinkles from the rocks, his quick eye and darting hand belying his apparent age. He straightened to answer Brendan's enquiry about the ruin, and replied in a soft north County Dublin accent.

'It was an old house years ago, all pullt down.' He looked inland towards the cluster of walls and trees. 'A man be the name of Filgate, Captain Filgate; he was an old extinguished officer or something. That's who lived there, yeh. There was a lot of people worked there in the old days. I don't remember it, but the older men around would.' These last words were said without a blink, although there could not have been too many older than himself in the area.

'There was a big farm o' land there wan time, and that's the house.' Later reading confirmed that the ruined house, called Lowther Lodge on the old maps, had been owned by a Mr Filgate in 1801. A map of 1870 showed it to have been a substantial establishment, with extensive walled gardens on the landward side, and it had the use of a small harbour in the tiny bay between the rocks.

I asked the man if he was getting many periwinkles.

'A good few,' he replied, but he was more interested in telling us about the area. He turned and pointed to a low mound further along the shore, 'That's more intrestin' over there. See that big hump of ground? That's an ancient site, yeh. It's all stone. You'd think it was grass from here, but if youse go up and have a look, it's all stone. I think it's an old grave; it's supposed to be related to the Knock, to the Knock graves.'

'Oh, Fourknocks,' said Brendan, referring to a well-known complex of passage graves a couple of miles inland. The man agreed. 'I was talking to a fella here a good few years ago. A very old man, and he told me that hump was very important; that's what he said, but I didn't know anything about it, but then I got intrested, and I looked it up, and on the old maps it's Knockward Hill. Yeh, it's an ancient ould spot that.'

We thanked him and headed across the rocks towards the mound perched at the edge of the sea. From its grassy top, we could see that we were on a little headland. In spite of the fact that the top of the mound was only a few metres above sea-level, there were long views inland, as well as to the north and south, owing to the low-lying nature of the coast. To the south, the islands off Skerries were strung along the sea horizon, and in the foreground the town of Balbriggan defined the edge of the Irish Sea.

The mound, which had a diameter of about fifteen metres, was indeed formed of boulders, which could be seen in places where the thin skin of turf had been disturbed. It looked indeed as if it might have been a cairn of stones raised over the tomb of prominent persons during the Neolithic or the Bronze Age. A broad crater in the top of the cairn was what remained, I later discovered, of excavations carried out by George Hamilton, a local landowner, early in the nineteenth century. He had found under the cairn a 'vast heap of human bones in a calcined state', set on a platform of hard, kneaded clay. This discovery led to the belief that it had been the burial place of the fallen in some great battle. In the centre of the cairn Hamilton found a chamber of huge flagstones, inside which was a basin fashioned from sandstone and surrounded by burnt bones.

We headed south towards distant Balbriggan, crunching our way across swathes of mussel and limpet shells, their shining insides turned up towards the sun like brittle flowers. A grassy bank running down to the shore was a mass of primroses and violets, seeming to thrive on the salty air, and to echo Spenser's lines:

> *And Primroses greene*
> *Embellish the sweete Violet*

The primrose for me is the herald of summer; I love its palest of yellows, washed in green, and its delicate perfume, which can fill the air of a warm spring day. At the base of the bank, great clumps of common scurvy grass sported masses of white flowers, which made me wonder, as always, why such a pretty plant has such an unattractive name.

An indignant wren scolded us from low boulder-clay cliffs, and, as we rounded a headland of pointed rocks, a dark, shining head rose steadily from the rolling swell a few metres from the shore, and eyed us curiously. I fumbled to get my camera out and focus on the animal; I have rarely seen seals close-up, but Brendan told me that they are a familiar sight to those who live along this part of the coast. Ireland has two species of seal, the common and the grey, of which the grey is the most common! Grey seals breed on nearby Lambay Island, but the seal taking an interest in us had a face not unlike that of a dog, and was probably a common seal.

The animal obligingly kept its head steady in the water until I had taken a good photograph, and then, without a splash, it was gone. I watched for a while to see if it would resurface, but in vain.

I hurried to catch up with Brendan, who had reached a beach of firm sand which followed a line of cliffs to the town of Balbriggan. Megan ranged back and forth, still tirelessly nosing the ground. To the south-east the islands off Skerries led the eye to a pair of bare rocks on the horizon, one topped with a slender, needle-like lighthouse. These outcrops of granite, the most northerly outliers of the Leinster granite field, are called the Rockabills, and are home to the largest surviving colony of roseate terns in Ireland. The lighthouse was completed in 1860 after a series of wrecks along this coast, culminating in the disaster of the *John Tayleur* in 1854.

It is difficult to envisage today how different matters at sea were at that time. Marine engines were troublesome, and ships depending on sail were at the mercy of wind and weather. If a vessel got into difficulties, communication between ship and shore was almost non-existent, and there was no lifeboat service in operation.

The iron-hulled *John Tayleur*, completed early in 1854 to an advanced design, had set out from Liverpool, bound for Australia, with nearly five hundred passengers. Contrary gale-force winds had forced the ship westwards, and it is said that the compasses were affected adversely by the iron hull, leaving the captain unsure of his position. To make matters worse, many of the crew were inexperienced Chinese and did not speak English, and the officers were unable to make their orders understood. Nearly forty-eight hours after leaving Liverpool, in hazy conditions and carrying too much sail, the vessel was driven towards Lambay Island. Only when breakers were spotted was an attempt made to alter course, but it was too late. Anchors were dropped to halt the inexorable drift towards destruction, but the force of the wind was such that the cables snapped. The hull of the ship was breached as it violently struck a reef under the eastern cliffs of Lambay, and it immediately began to sink by the stern. The passengers and crew panicked in the midst of all the turmoil: while some escaped by simply leaping on to the shore, many were swept off the deck by the rising sea and dashed against the rocks. Others scrambled desperately into the rigging, and a number saved themselves by crossing to dry land on fallen spars. Of the two hundred and fifty women and children on board, only three survived, while forty men were drowned. Of the two hundred and eighty-two survivors to make it to safety, five were found to have been stowaways!

Megan came running to us with a large dead rat in her mouth. Brendan took up a master's stance, arms akimbo, and in a firm scolding tone told her to drop it. I cowered away from the spray of sand thrown up as she shook the corpse vigorously, threw it up in the air and caught it again, then offered it to her master. In fact, she did everything but drop it. After assuming a theatrically stern expression and trying again several times without success, Brendan gave up and walked on. Megan continued joyfully after us, almost polishing our heels with the dreaded rodent.

Six-metre-high cliffs of boulder clay towered over us as we proceeded along the beach towards Balbriggan, defined by the sharp pinnacle of a church spire. The cliffs are interrupted at the end of the beach by a Martello tower and a Victorian coastguard boat-house, both in a regrettable state of neglect and decay, with a blue limestone-paved slipway polished smooth from use. Beside it was an old store, which once probably housed a breeches-buoy cart, used in the nineteenth century for rescuing people from ships that had been driven on to the shore.

The north–south railway line runs on a high rampart above the beach, blocking any view of the town. We followed it until it crossed Balbriggan Harbour by way of a high stone viaduct of eleven arches. One of the great arches shelters what appears to be an ornate Victorian lifeboat-house dated 1889, but its doors mysteriously face inland. What remains of the river that used to run into the sea at this point has been turned into a decorative canal, a miniature version of

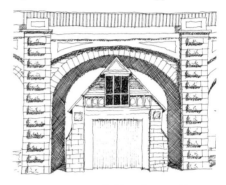

Lifeboat-house Balbriggan

the fine mall in Westport, County Mayo, with weirs and bridges. Unfortunately, its beauty seems to be ignored, but its utility as a repository of supermarket trolleys and beer cans appears to be much appreciated by some of the local populace.

Balbriggan was once so renowned for its cotton hosiery that the town's name became a generic term for high quality stockings. There had been a cottage cotton industry in the area around Balbriggan early in the eighteenth century, but George Hamilton, the amateur archaeologist who had excavated the prehistoric graves, was responsible for many improvements in the town in the late 1700s, and helped to organise the industry. The cotton and stocking factories and the dye works that he set up became the mainstay of employment in the area for nearly two hundred years. The wearing of cotton stockings was fashionable throughout the eighteenth and early nineteenth centuries, but eventually new materials became more popular, and although the company diversified, it finally had to close its doors in 1980.

Balbriggan Harbour, originally built in the late eighteenth century as part of the upgrading of the town, today sadly displays its decline with a cluster of small, rusty, net-festooned trawlers with names like *Santa Lucia, Girl Margaret* and *Atlantic Breeze,* and derelict craft that are tied to, or lean against, its pier. In the open hold of a broad-beamed, filthy boat from Brittany, two blackened men were working on the engine, surrounded by a chaos of old parts. Their heavy-limbed shuffling about in the squalor suggested that they did not really believe they would ever get the thing fixed; their white faces looked almost appealingly up and out at us from the darkness.

We walked around the harbour and passed through an ancient narrow and winding little street, where I would not have been surprised to meet Jim Hawkins. Then we descended to the shore again and crunched along a beach of limestone pebbles. The tide was coming in, and as the beach gave way to low cliffs, we barely made it to a grassy path ascending further on to the clifftop. Here we found a terrace of stolid Victorian houses overlooking the sea. Their outlook was magnificent: a great expanse of uninterrupted Irish Sea glistened in the foreground, while to the north the sun sculpted the many summits of the Mournes.

Our path passed through a rough gap in a stone wall, and we stepped suddenly out of the 1880s and into the 1990s to find ourselves in the middle of a semi-detached housing estate. Between the houses and the cliffs, a county council tractor was trawling up and down a broad stretch of what is referred to on planning application maps as 'Public Open Space'. These unfortunate expanses of sterile, fertiliser-green grass, which require regular and expensive mechanical mowing, might as well be 'outer space' for all the use they are to the public!

We left suburban Balbriggan behind and, as we followed the cliffs southwards, I made out ahead, on a wooded hill, the neo-Gothic towers of Ardgillan Castle. Our route along the clifftop had taken us, before we realised it, across the bottoms of a couple of very long, private gardens, but after making our way through a cabbage field, we reached a well-developed hedge that successfully blocked our progress. We followed the hedge inland through cabbages and leeks to reach the public road near an old pedestrian bridge that spanned both the road and the railway line beside it.

The bridge was originally built by the Dublin and Drogheda Railway Company in 1844. When the railway line was being planned, the Taylors of Ardgillan owned the land down to the seashore, where they had a swimming place, and although the problem might have been circumvented by building a buttressed embankment along the shore, it would have been a most uneconomical solution. Instead, based on precedents established during the construction of the first railway line to be built in Ireland, the Dublin to Kingstown (Dun Laoghaire) Railway, completed in 1834, an accommodation was arrived at with the Taylors to cross their land. As part of the agreement, the railway company undertook to build this pedestrian bridge which gives continued access to the swimming cove, and arranged that all trains would stop briefly at a private station in the demesne to pick up and drop off passengers. Although the descendants of the Taylors moved out in the 1960s and trains no longer stop here, Iarnród Éireann continues to maintain the footbridge; it is a pity, though, to see that recent works to the bridge are far from being in keeping with what remains of the Victorian original.

Brendan took me to see the old Taylor swimming place, off the road and down a narrow leafy pathway. We descended steeply to the rocky shore by way of a cast-iron balustraded staircase, cut from the limestone bedrock, called the Lady's Stairs. It is so called because it is said that the ghost of a Victorian lady, who drowned in the cove below, is often seen there. At the bottom of the cliff is a ruined bathing pavilion overlooking a smooth flat rock washed by the waves of a high tide. It was easy to picture a Victorian picnic party here: the heavily moustached men in their straw boaters and striped blazers, and the women in long, many-layered skirts, their white flowery hats keeping their pinned-up hair in place.

The high tide made it impossible to continue along the shore, so we had to climb back up to the road. A little further on, the mock turrets and battlements of Ardgillan Castle, backed by a thick wood, came into sight a half-mile inland. It is not really a castle, but a Georgian country house, built in 1738 by the Reverend Robert Taylor. He was a grandson of Thomas Taylor, who came to Ireland in 1653 as Deputy Surveyor to Sir William Petty, the author of the Down Survey, and took part in the first comprehensive and accurate mapping of the country. The new maps he helped to devise were soon put to practical use, ensuring the efficient seizure of the lands of Irish Catholics who had supported the Confederate side in the recent wars, and their redistribution to Cromwell's soldiers and loyal supporters. In 1660, Taylor bought twenty-one thousand acres of land in Ireland and settled in County Meath, holding a succession of important governmental positions until his death in 1682. His grandson Robert purchased a stretch of wooded land (the name Ardgillan comes from the Gaelic *Ard Coille* or High Wood) between Balbriggan and Skerries in 1721. Using retired soldiers and itinerant labourers who were paid a penny and one meal a day for their work, Robert Taylor had much of the land cleared of trees and built a modest, two-storey country house, originally called 'Prospect'. Around 1815 the house was much added to and 'improved' with the addition of turrets and battlements that were the fashion of the time, and it was given the name 'Ardgillan Castle'.

The Taylor family were in residence at Ardgillan for two hundred and twenty years. Many of them had distinguished military careers: one was a general at the battle of Waterloo, another in the battle of Alma in the Crimean War and the recapture of Lucknow in 1858 during the Indian Mutiny, and a third served in the Sudan, the Boer War and World War I. Because of the financial difficulties of running a large estate, the family were forced to sell Ardgillan in 1962, and it came into the possession of Dublin County Council in 1981. The council now operates the eighty-hectare demesne of mixed woodland and gardens as a regional park, and the castle has been restored and opened to visitors.

We made our way along the road that follows the cliffs towards Skerries, and soon came to a cove called Barnagaorach where we dropped down to the shore again, and followed a blue-grey limestone breakwater. Frequently we had to leap and dash ahead as waves crashed at our feet and the tide surged noisily up the shingle. Megan found a new toy in a large and long-dead curlew, and ran beside us shaking it so that its bony wings extended and flexed as if the bird were about to take off. No amount of scolding and finger-wagging by her master would make her drop this new plaything.

As we rounded a corner, the cluster of buildings lining the harbour at Red Island, a low-lying piece of land connected to Skerries by a narrow isthmus, came into view. Their bright and cheerful colours, across a foreground of a rolling sea that had taken on a turquoise tint, gave the scene a Mediterranean look.

Red Island

We followed the road into Skerries along the shingly North Strand, on to which great thundering breakers were crashing. The strand lines a fine crescent-shaped bay, overlooked by houses and old stone sheds which used to serve the harbour in its nineteenth-century heyday. The sheds are built with Milverton limestone, an excellent quality stone from nearby quarries. It used to be exported to England from the harbour here, and older residents of Skerries remember stacks of it, like terraces of two-storey houses, along the quayside, awaiting transportation.

At that time, Skerries was the home port for a considerable number of small cargo vessels that traded around the British Isles, and much further afield too. A local captain named Edwards had a three-masted schooner of one hundred and thirty-six gross tons, and a description of just one of his voyages in 1898 gives an idea of the sort of trade that turned Skerries from a little fishing village into a place of some substance. His first trip of the year began when he sailed for Cardiff to collect a cargo of coal for Cadiz in southern Spain. There he loaded the schooner with salt for St John's, Newfoundland, and crossed the Atlantic in thirty days. He unloaded one hundred tons at St John's, and then sailed north, crossing the straits of Belle Isle to reach Indian Harbour, an island in the estuary of the Churchill river in western Labrador, where he discharged the balance. At White Bear Island he loaded with cod, and after calling at two more ports to make up a full load, sailed east to Gibraltar, making the crossing in twenty-four days. From Gibraltar he sailed into the Mediterranean to the port of Genoa, and then on to Catania in Sicily, where he took on board a cargo of sulphur for Almeria in Spain. From there he sailed to Bona in Algeria and loaded oak-bark for Limerick, which finally brought him home.

I suppose World War I and technological progress put an end to the adventurous voyages of skippers like Captain Edwards. In the little harbour where once a forest of schooner masts reached towards the sky, a scattering of tired old fishing craft moved languidly on their moorings, worrying their fetters — modern nylon ropes knotted around ancient iron rings embedded in the pier.

The harbour road we were following and the houses and pubs fronting on to it are built on a narrow moraine of gravel, called the Dorn, which was once all that connected Red Island, no longer distinguishable as a geographic entity, to the mainland. Formerly called Havan Island, it became known as Red Island comparatively recently, and there are a number of theories as to where the 'Red' came from. One suggests that the island was used to spread out and dry sailcloth that had been treated with a preservative made of tree-bark and cutch, a type of pitch, that gave the material a rust-red colour. There is evidence that a 'barking yard' was established in the town in the early eighteenth century which would bear this out. An account of 1859 describes Red Island as amounting to 'about nine acres of ground, which in springtime is covered by an exquisite carpet of wildflowers, whereon rabbits disport and gambol in the most amusing manner'.

As we walked along the harbour Brendan pointed out, lying in an alley to the side of the Waterfront Restaurant, a great timber spar from a sailing schooner. A massive piece of timber, it had once hung on one of the masts of the schooner *John Patton*, wrecked near Balbriggan in 1881, and it brings home to one the scale of these great sailing ships, and how shipping technology has changed over the last century.

Joe Mays's little pub further down the harbour drew us in, and we sat, stretched our legs and had a glass of stout each. I was relieved to see that Megan had given up the curlew, and she became quite civilised, taking up a position under the bench on which we sat, her head on her paws, watching. Besides the barman, there were two other occupants, fishermen I guessed — one a great bear of a man with a patent peaked cap, and the other a slight figure with a lined and weather-beaten face. They were engaged in a very serious conversation, during which each had lengthy points to make, the big man emphasising his with gentle thumps of his big fist on the bar. I strained to hear what they were discussing so earnestly, sure that it must have to do with the high seas and storms and the state of the fishing fleet in Skerries, but I was disappointed when it finally became clear, from the odd word I picked up, that they were discussing the local soccer team!

We finished our drinks and went out again to the harbour front, making our way around to Red Island's Martello tower. The circular fort was built on the highest point of the island in the early 1800s, within signal distance of other towers at Balbriggan to the north and Shenick's Island to the south. It was put to unusual use in the 1950s and '60s when it became a dormitory for the staff of the Red Island Holiday Camp, which encompassed most of the island. Among those who lived in the tower for a couple of months every summer were the comedian Hal Roche, entertainments manager for the camp for a number of years, and Senator Feargal Quinn, who as a teenager did holiday work in the camp.

The holiday camp was opened in 1947 by Eamonn Quinn, Feargal's father. Holiday camps were all the rage after the war, particularly in Britain, giving a new and lucrative use to disused army camps and even prisoner-of-war camps where the 'huts' became 'chalets', and multitudes were provided with cheap, organised holidays away from home.

Eamonn Quinn cornered part of this market, arranging all-in holidays which included travel to Ireland by air or sea. His policy was to concentrate on value for money and to get his visitors to return again and again. He claimed that as soon as his patrons entered Red Island and paid for their holiday, they did not have to put their hands in their pockets again until they had left. Feargal Quinn told me that this policy of his father's was the inspiration for his own 'boomerang principle', which he later adopted in his highly successful supermarket chain: the practice of concentrating on getting customers to come back again, rather than just serving them once.

Eamonn Quinn did not like the idea of chalets, and had the architect Vincent Gallagher design a building that housed two hundred and fifty bedrooms, a ballroom, a theatre and a licensed bar under one roof. A staff of over a hundred from all parts of Ireland worked in the camp; they were recruited annually by Eamonn Quinn himself, who would travel from town to town holding interviews. He was more concerned, in the people he hired, with a pleasant personality than a high level of efficiency. So far-flung were the places from which recruits were selected, Feargal Quinn recalls that there were times when new staff had great difficulty understanding each other's regional accents!

As well as the recruitment of staff, Eamonn Quinn did his own marketing, having seventy thousand leaflets printed each year and travelling around the working-men's clubs of Lancashire, Yorkshire and Cheshire, selling his holidays. In the early days, the plentiful food available in Ireland was a great draw for the British, who were still enduring post-war rationing. By the late 1950s, Red Island was a household name in Britain, and aeroplanes were being chartered to fly in holiday-makers.

Plans for expanding and improving the holiday camp were on the drawing board in 1971, when a week's holiday at the high season, including travel, cost twenty-five pounds, but the Northern Ireland troubles were looming. The burning of the British Embassy in Dublin in February 1972 was the beginning of the end of the holiday camp on Red Island; the numbers were drastically down that season, and later in the year they had to close. The camp is still fondly remembered by Skerries people; apart from the valuable holiday employment it provided, many local people still reminisce on the exciting holiday romances the camp brought them.

We wandered around to the Captain's Bathing Place on the south side of Red Island, an early tourist amenity developed by The Skerries Visitors Association in 1902. Offshore to the east, surf-fringed, was low-lying Colt Island, and beyond it, with its tiny ruined oratory, St Patrick's Island. St Patrick is said to have stayed for a time on St Patrick's Island, and there has been a monastic settlement there since early Christian times, when it was accessible on foot at low tides. It had withstood a number of sackings by the Vikings, and in 1148, an important synod was held there, presided over by Gelasius, the Primate of Ireland, and attended by St Malachy. After the synod, Malachy travelled to Rome to consult with Pope Eugene III, but died on the way, at Clairvaux. By 1220 the sea had washed away the causeway, and the monastery had been abandoned and re-established on the mainland at Holmpatrick.

Near the Bathing Place, the print of St Patrick's foot is said to be preserved on the surface of a rock by the shore. Robbers from Skerries apparently stole the saint's goat, and to apprehend them, he leapt in one great bound from the island across to the mainland, where the mark of his landing was preserved for all time on the rocky shore. I wondered if this was why, apparently, if you want to insult a Skerries person, you call him a Skerries Goat.

We were unable to find the mark of St Patrick's landing, and as we searched the shoreline, the sea turned grey and then a metallic gun-barrel shade scattered with heaving white horses, as great black rain-filled clouds came bearing down from the north-west. Leaving Red Island behind, we made our way by South Beach towards Brendan's home in the centre of town.

It was clear from our day's walk that the Dublin coast could be closely followed, and in addition there was a wealth of history, flora and fauna to be gleaned from it. It had been an enjoyable introduction, and it was easy for me to decide to walk the rest of the way to Bray. I made arrangements to start the following week, but, as it turned out, these plans had to be postponed, and it was not until the autumn that I was able to return to Skerries and continue where I had left off.

2

Skerries to Portrane

On a glorious September morning I returned to Skerries and set out along the beach that extends southwards from the town. A large flock of oyster-catchers arrayed along the water's edge were piping warning calls as I approached, before taking to the air in a cloud and wheeling around over the waves and alighting behind me. The tide seemed to be out, but, being unfamiliar with the beach, I could not tell if was rising or falling. I would have to keep an eye on it, because for much of the stretch I planned to walk that day, to the village of Portrane, I would have to follow the shore. In spite of a sunny start to the day, thunder showers were forecast, but I was hoping they would hold off for at least a couple of hours.

At the southern end of the beach, I came across broad expanses of bedrock shining damply between green patches of seaweed and pools that mirrored the sky. Great numbers of gulls, curlews and turnstones moved among the pools to harvest the molluscs and worms offered up by the tide. The rocks proved as hazardous to cross as the ankle-deep lakes of thick-trunked oarweeds that lay between them. Two hundred years ago many of the poor peasants of the Fingal coast survived on the pittance they earned by the back-breaking labour of gathering this seaweed and burning it to produce that porous ash from which iodine is manufactured.

At the back of the beach, under a cliff of glacial till, the rock was sufficiently weed-free to see that it was a limestone, blue in colour, with a smooth undulating surface. In places it was strongly reminiscent of Burren pavements, except here the bedding plane was greatly tilted towards the east, a result of some primordial subterranean upheaval. The tide-line, paved in sponge-like perforated cobbles of limestone, was scattered with a collection of colourful flotsam, including plastic bottles, lengths of jute and nylon rope, and great clumps of fishing net that looked like hanks of hair from a giant's head.

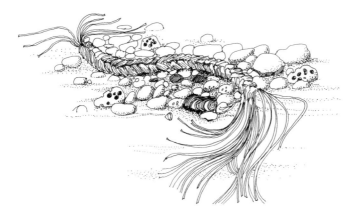

I rounded a promontory at the end of the beach, and crossed a barbed wire fence carried by railway sleepers right down to the tide line. Beyond the fence I was able to enjoy the comfort of soft grass underfoot as I crossed a field that sloped down to the shore. As the town of Skerries receded from sight behind the promontory, Lambay Island came into view ahead, dark and featureless against an ominous black sky, laden with rain-bearing clouds. Yet another flock of birds rose in front from where they had been gathered on the rocks — this time about fifty lapwings, squealing eerily as they flapped in an ungainly scatter to settle again further along the shore.

Soon I had to leave the comfort of the grassy field behind as a hedge diverted me on to the rocky shore where I walked under low cliffs of boulder clay. The surroundings reminded me of the last time I had walked this way, some years before. I had been on a field trip with an extra-mural study group taking a course in geology at University College Dublin. It was cold that day, bitterly cold, and as we crouched together in the lee of the cliffs, drinking mugs of coffee from thermos flasks, something colourful caught my eye among the rocks at the water's edge. It was a large piece of white plywood, on which was painted in red letters: 'If the klaxon sounds an intermittent signal, prepare to leave. If the klaxon sounds a continuous signal, clear the area immediately.' The others gathered around and we discussed what the sign could mean. We decided that it must be from a nuclear power-station, a warning of the emergency signals that would be given in the event of an accident, and a leak of radioactive gases. It brought home to us the proximity of Britain's nuclear threat; further research suggested that the plywood had floated across the Irish Sea from a power-station on the north coast of Anglesey, a little more than sixty miles from the Dublin coast.

I mounted the cliffs and was soon surprised to see, not far ahead, the roof-tops of the village of Loughshinny. Looking back the way I had come, something I take a great pleasure in doing when I am walking any distance, I realised that St Patrick's Island could still be seen off Skerries; away beyond it, the blue silhouette of the Mournes made an undulating horizon with the sea. My eyes ranged over the disturbed clay ahead as I walked across a harrowed field, because I always expect to find something thrown up on to the surface of the ground that has been lying undisturbed in the darkness below. Visual surveys of this sort have become a standard archaeological technique for the non-invasive assessment of large areas of agricultural land — modern ploughing and harrowing reach deep into the topsoil, exposing levels that have not seen daylight for many centuries.

I did find something, not a rich jewel or ornament, but a beautiful piece of craftsmanship nevertheless, something that in its day certainly amounted to a valuable possession. It was protruding from a lump of clay, its pale colour catching my eye. I stopped, and extracted from the soil a flat piece of flint that would cover the palm of your hand. Flint, a hard, siliceous mineral that occurs naturally in  chalky limestones in Counties Antrim and Derry, was the mainstay of the Stone Age; it could be shattered or 'knapped' into extremely sharp tools of different shapes — arrowheads, knives or scrapers, which were used to skin animals or prepare animal pelts for tanning. Nodules of flint that were deposited by the ice-sheet during glaciation are frequently found along the east coast of Ireland, but this was not a nodule or a naturally broken piece. It had the marks of having been knapped, giving it a sharpened edge on one side, and was most likely a scraping tool of some kind. I was probably the first human to hold this artefact for more than three thousand years.

With my 'find' tucked into my knapsack, I continued along the edge of the field, marvelling at the bedrock lining the shore. It was a composition of undulating zig-zag forms — ideal graphic examples of geological folding — for which Loughshinny is well-known to geologists. A cobbled lane took me into the hamlet's cluster of tiny cottages. It was once a very poor place, and the quaint character it has today is largely attributable to the tiny house plots and the organic way in which the village developed around the shore of the inlet. This framework should give Loughshinny all the makings of a picturesque seaside village

21

reminiscent of villages of similar size in Devon and Cornwall, if the local authority insisted that individual developments were designed with sensitivity and concern for context. This has plainly not been the case, and, in addition to a considerable improvement in local economic conditions, a stricter policy on behalf of the planning department will be needed before improvements will be seen in Loughshinny.

In Loughshinny

As I raised my camera to photograph one of the few remaining thatched cottages, a large woman came out of the door dressed in a shapeless green shift, a towel around her head. She beamed and asked, 'Are ye goin' to take me picture?'

I could hardly refuse! She drew herself up, put her hands on her hips, and I took her photograph.

'There y'are now,' she said, as if she had given me a present, and I suppose in a way she had. I thanked her and, as she watched, followed a grassy walk along the back of the beach past a row of summer chalets and cottages. The cliffs on the western side of the beach consist of astonishing plastic folds of metamorphosed limestone; it takes little imagination to conceive of the great forces and heat that must have been brought to bear aeons ago to create these massive wrinkles.

I climbed a path to the clifftop and walked towards Loughshinny's Martello tower, which stands at the seaward end of a broad headland called Drimminagh Point. About two thousand years ago, during the Iron Age, a series of great ditches and banks were constructed between the headland and the mainland, creating what is known as a promontory fort. Earthworks survive for a surprising length of time; the fosses, or ditches, are still over a metre deep and the banks are in places over two metres high. Even today, if a timber palisade were erected on top of the bank, it would provide a formidable defensive fortification. In recent years, finds of a shard of Roman pottery and a couple of second-century Roman coins on the headland suggest that, in conjunction with the sheltered harbour of Loughshinny, this may have been a place of some importance two millennia ago. The configuration of the defensive earthworks could suggest that it may even have been a trading outpost of Roman Britain.

Further vague shapes in the grassy surface of the promontory indicated there were once other structures here, and I made my way out to the tower following one of them, a slightly raised strip of ground which nurtured the only thistles in the entire field. I assumed that this particular earthwork might have been the military access road for the transport of the building materials and subsequently the great twenty-four-pounder gun and its ammunition, but later research indicated that it also was of Iron Age origin.

The Martello towers, which occur frequently along the Leinster and Munster coasts, were built between 1804 and 1815; on the Dublin coast there were originally twelve such towers in addition to a number of batteries. The idea of these comparatively small structures mounting a single rotating twenty-four pounder gun being used for coastal defence seems to have come from the

Mediterranean. In 1794 a single such tower garrisoned by a small French force had successfully repulsed a British naval attack on Cap Mortella in Corsica, wreaking considerable damage on the seventy-four-gun ship of the line, *Fortitude*, and the thirty-two-gun frigate *Juno*, forcing them to withdraw to sea. The British were so impressed by this action that they adopted the idea, and similar towers were built to defend the coast of Minorca, and subsequently the British Isles, against French attack. Each of the structures cost eighteen hundred pounds and had a garrison of six to eight men. The guns, which can still be found in place on a couple of the towers in the southwest of Ireland, had a range of about a mile. They were never fired in anger, however, and after the battle of Waterloo the garrisons were withdrawn, although some soldiers are recorded as living in the towers as late as 1867.

The tower at Drimminagh still retains most of its original plaster and some of its cast-iron window frames. I was surprised to find a stone-built structure on its seaward side that, exposed as it was, could only have been a privy! Perhaps this is a survival from the post-French wars occupations.

To the south there was a new vista to take in: the next promontory at Rush, topped by another Martello tower, and a rash of housing that has spread out from the village in recent years. In the distance beyond Rush I could see the strange juxtaposed round tower and the water tower at Portrane, and further east, looming out of the dark haze, the shape of Howth Head. Curtains of rain were sweeping eastwards, but so far they had not come north, and I was walking in warm sunshine, although the very calmness of the sea seemed to threaten bad weather.

I climbed down to a tiny gravelly beach, called 'Brooks End' on my 1870 map, and sat to take a rest, basking in what I thought would be the last of the sun. All around were tiny pieces of worn glass among the pebbles — blue, green, brown and red gems catching the sun's rays. These rounded shards of old glass were not in just one area of the beach, but were distributed evenly across it. I subsequently searched for records of shipwrecks in the area, and in Edward Bourke's *Shipwrecks of the Irish Coast* (1994) could come up with only two possible candidates for such a distribution of broken glass on this beach: a ship with a cargo of wine, which is said to have gone down near Portmarnock in 1464, and a schooner called the *Dolly Arden*, which sank near Rush in 1900. I could find no references to 'Brook' and what kind of 'end' was referred to in the place-name.

I walked on refreshed, ascending gently to the cliffs, and came to a place where the land turned abruptly west. I had reached the southern extremity of a great field of metamorphosed limestone that extended back to Loughshinny. The south-facing edge was formed of almost vertical sheets of rock, making the cliff resemble a massive man-made retaining wall. Beyond, where before there had been only glacial till, the sea had eroded the shoreline westwards, thus creating Rush beach.

A quarter of a mile inland was a modern housing development, roofs festooned with television aerials, but in the middle of this mass of concrete roof tiles, and rising high above them, stood a tall six-columned Corinthian portico, as elegant in appearance as it was incongruous in its location. This sad monument is all that remains of the 'big house' of this area, Kenure Park, a mid-eighteenth-century mansion remodelled in the 1840s by the architect George Papworth. The historian Samuel Lewis said of this substantial three-storeyed house in 1834: 'The mansion is spacious and handsome, and contains many good apartments, a collection of paintings by the first masters, and a selection of vases and other relics from the remains of Pompeii collected by the late Mr Palmer when he was in Italy.' The Palmers sold the house in 1964 and it fell into disrepair over the ensuing years. In 1978 it was torn down by the local authority in just two days, and its overgrown gardens, rich in exotic species, were levelled by bulldozers. The portico was spared, thanks to the efforts of the local conservation group, but I am not sure that was a good idea. It reminds me a little of the grisly mummified arm of the famous nineteenth-century prize-fighter John Donnelly, which for years was displayed in a glass case in a pub in County Kildare.

I found a steep gully that took me down the cliffs on to the broad, clean beach, lined with a collection of beach houses, some that were timber-built chalets with verandas at the front, others that had once been mobile homes but which had now graduated to better things by means of subtly added extensions and excrescences. One or two had real character and were surrounded by well-kept if tiny gardens. I could not help wondering about the legal status of some of these holiday homes. In one place, a new, substantial and expensively built house just behind the beach, had, sandwiched between it and the sands, a mobile home and a dilapidated shack on a postage-stamp platform of earth.

The name Rush is derived from *Ros Eo*, the Promontory of the Yews. There were no yew trees to be seen, but there may have been when a fishing village grew up here in the sixteenth century. The place became well known for its salted cod and ling, and indeed in more recent times for its cod liver oil.

In the early days, income from fishing had been augmented by smuggling, an almost respectable occupation in most coastal areas in the mid to late eighteenth century. The illicit importation of tea, brandy and tobacco were the mainstay of a trade that occupied as many as fifty vessels based in Rush at that time. The names of many of the smugglers lived on in the folk memory here for many years, and none more so than that of Luke Ryan. He was born near Rush in 1750, and as a young man emigrated to France, where he was commissioned as a lieutenant in an Irish regiment of the French Army. He must have gained sea-going experience in his early days in Rush, because he soon found himself commanding a privateer named *The Black Prince*, with which he returned to the Irish Sea and combined piracy with smuggling during the prolonged wars between France and England.

The Black Prince was a formidable craft, carrying an armament of eighteen six-pounder cannon, and with it Luke Ryan captured more English prizes than any other privateer of the period, most of which he brought to Roscoff in Brittany to be sold. Arrested by the English in 1781, he was tried for piracy at the Old Bailey and sentenced to death, but he obtained a pardon through the efforts of the French court during a brief peace between the two countries. He accumulated a nest-egg of seventy thousand pounds, a fortune at the time, but his French bankers pocketed the money, and he died in 1789 in the King's Bench debtors' prison in London, where he had been detained for a debt of two hundred pounds.

The village of Rush extends along a main street for two miles inland from the harbour, and was, until the 1960s, a very handsome place because of the large number of thatched houses it contained. At the time of my visit there were only fourteen left, well scattered about the town. I came to the harbour and, crossing the road, went into the Harbour Bar for a glass of Guinness. It was empty except for two at the end of the bar: an elderly man drinking a stout and a chaser, and a thin young man nursing a cup of coffee.

A cheerful barman took my order and I admired the photographs on the wall of prize catches made by members of the local angling club. One face, obviously that of the local champion, appeared in the majority of pictures, in each proudly holding aloft his latest victim. In one of the photographs he posed with a huge and ugly-looking fish. I asked the men at the end of the bar what it was.

The younger man said something like 'a boulabas'.

'A boulabas?' I repeated, more than asked, having never heard of such a fish.

'Yeh, a boulabas, that's what it is, yeh.'

I gazed at the photo again and marvelled at the size of the creature. Boulabas sounded a bit like bouillabaisse, a French chowder, but the man could have hardly meant that.

'Can you eat it?'

'Nah. It's like a big bird-dog, or a dogfish, but a different race,' the older man explained.

'What would you catch it with?'

'A big lump of mackerel, you'd need, an a big hook.'

I was not sure if they were having me on, although they seemed perfectly serious. They went on to converse between themselves, the older man saying, 'I wouldn't be fuckin' bothered goin' out in a little boat to catch fish,' and the younger man replying, 'And what do you fuckin' do with them when you catch them — fuckin' throw 'em back in again.'

I swallowed my glass of stout in two long draughts, and thanking the barman, returned to the street wondering still about the 'boulabas'.

I was pleasantly surprised to find that the sun had come out and was shining strongly from a sky that had lost its ominous clouds; only white cotton-wool-like puffs were left behind by the dark front that had disappeared eastwards over the Irish Sea.

Near the harbour, in the middle of a colourful flower-bed, stood a beautiful hand-operated water pump, one of the rarer panelled and decorated rectangular types, dating from about 1850, although its condition was almost as new. These pumps predate the more common circular sort, and their design was directly based on the previous model pumps, which were made from a squared elm log hollowed out with an auger. I know of a few of these original wooden public pumps that are still standing at roadside locations in the Dublin area, although they must be more than one hundred and fifty years old. Rural water pumps are among the last surviving pieces of roadside 'furniture' of the Victorian era. Horse troughs, some with dog troughs incorporated, which were a common

Cast-iron pump at Rush

feature of streets in towns when I was a boy, are a thing of the past, and although no longer in working order, it is good to see a few of the old pumps being conserved in their original locations.

I stood to admire the various colourful small craft leaning against the pier and beached on the sand in the low tide. One was a long, open boat, with a 'bow' front fore and aft, and looked as if at one time it might have been a lifeboat on an ocean-going liner. A man came out of one of the little cottages beside the pier, followed by a black-and-white mongrel. He had a rugged, 'lived in' face, and was dressed as if he were auditioning for a part in a dramatisation of *The Ancient Mariner*, in a grey, hand-knitted gansey and heavy canvas trousers stuffed into rubber boots. To complete the picture, he clenched an old scarred pipe in his jaw. If anyone would know the history of the 'lifeboat', I reckoned it would be this man.

He stopped at my question and put his fists on his hips.

'I think that was an ould lobster boat. I don't know,' he answered in a soft north County Dublin accent. 'It probably was a lifeboat originally alright; it has nice lines on it. I don't think it will be doin' much more cruisin' — it's there a long time now. Are you goin' to photograph it, are you?'

And then, looking at my knapsack, he said, 'They're givin' bad weather. Are ye walkin'?'

I told him I was walking to Portrane.

'You must be able to walk, alright; you must be a fit man. It's a great hobby. It's a pity there's not more people at it. What way will you go?'

I told him I was following the coast, but hoped to be able to shorten my journey by crossing the railway embankment at Rogerstown; did he know if it were possible?

'That's right. You'll go over the viaduct; otherwise, you'd have to go up through Lusk an' all. Well, d'ye know, that's the way the fellas years ago used to go to work in Lambs' fruit farm: they used to go up the line on the bikes; it'd save them goin' up Turvey Avenue — that's what they used to do now. It was years ago, I remember fellas doin' that. There's a golf course there now.'

He took a puff on his pipe, and as he moved off, said, 'I hope the weather holds up for you now. Good luck with it!'

He whistled for the dog, which had been sniffing my boots and, giving me a wave, strolled slowly down the pier, the dog trotting behind. A minute later, I realised I had forgotten to ask him about the boulabas. I subsequently angled through all the literature I could find searching for this species of 'bird-dog', but without a bite, and pictures I found of dogfish had no resemblance to the great fish displayed in the photos on the pub wall, so the mystery remains.

I walked along a street past houses named 'Notre Dame', 'Sea Verge' and 'Tower View', the last named for the Martello tower that stands, incongruously, close to its original condition, in the house's back garden. The individual houses had little character and were typical of the architecture of the 1960s. I was disappointed with what I had seen of Rush; I suppose, like Loughshinny, its inhabitants were more concerned with survival and basic comforts than with retaining old, cold and draughty thatched cottages for the delight of travellers like me.

The houses thinned out, and I found myself walking along a narrow hedgeless road through fields of cabbages and sprouts, rabbits scurrying for cover ahead of me. Portrane's peninsula stretched across the horizon, and the bad weather that had threatened earlier on had moved away eastwards, leaving, with the exception of a dark Lambay Island, a sunny landscape in its wake. As soon as I could, I crossed a sandy field to reach the shore, glad to have the lapping sea-sounds of the rising tide and the piping of the oyster-catchers in my ears once more.

The towers of Portrane were about two miles away as the crow flies, but I knew that I would have to walk maybe three times that, around the Rogerstown inlet, before I would get closer to them. It was a relief to reach the long crescent of Rush's South Beach, after crossing a deep swamp of seaweed, and stride out along its firm sands that stretched a mile or so into the distance. The beach was scattered with a rich collection of seashells, including queen scallops, oysters, razor-shells, cockles, mussels and common whelks, many of the last very large but none complete. This incompleteness allowed glimpses of the whelks' usually hidden but beautiful interior, the broken external whorls revealing the polished delicacy of the mantle, a piece of sculptural perfection in the most delicate pastel shades.

At the back of the beach was a rampart of substantial sand-dunes, unexpectedly not occupied by mobile homes, probably because of a golf course on the far side. The only person I could see was a mile or so away, across the water on Portrane beach, an angler, probably fishing for bass.

It was almost one o'clock, and as soon as I had left all signs of habitation behind me, I sat on the warm sands to have my lunch. A gentle breeze textured the sea's surface, which glinted silver in the midday light. Except for a couple of short stops, I had been walking briskly all morning, and the water looked inviting. Apart from the lone angler in the distance, there was no one in sight, so I swiftly stripped off and trotted into the tide, expecting a bit of a shock. To my surprise, the water was not cold but coolly refreshing, and I ducked in head-first. Rolling over, I floated, arms outstretched, looking up at a sky scattered with white gossamer clouds while I regained my breath. After a few minutes I returned to the strand tingling all over, and dried off in the sun. It was with reluctance that I dressed again, hoisted my knapsack on my back and continued south.

Before long, I rounded the southern end of Rush beach, and the narrow isthmus between Rogerstown Pier and the 'burrow' of Portrane came into view. The shallow and sheltered Rogerstown inlet stretched into the distance to the west. Here, in the ninth century, Scandinavian seafarers dragged their boats up on to the sands, built wooden huts and settled in for the winter, rather than set out on the long return voyage to their homes. Similar winter bases in other parts of Ireland, such as Drogheda and Waterford, grew to be trading posts and eventually cities.

The Rogerstown inlet, called Rogershaven by those Scandinavian visitors, is one of four deep indentations that mark the coast of County Dublin. Three of these — the Broadmeadow estuary, the Baldoyle inlet and this at Rogerstown — are salt marshes shallowly covered twice daily by tides, and partially separated from the sea by substantial sand-dune peninsulas. The little swampy wildernesses provided by such conditions are not common around Ireland's coasts and are often dismissed as unproductive, with no other use than as suitable sites to dump a town's garbage. Their layers of sands, muds and water, however, are teeming with an abundance of hidden life: countless billions of tiny shellfish, shrimp-like creatures, and a variety of worms. In one square metre of ground, as many as a thousand of one species of tiny snail can be found. When the tide is out, these organisms, together with species of water plant such as eel-grass, provide an inexhaustible supply of feeding for water fowl and geese in surroundings where a predator cannot approach without being seen a long way off. Anyone with even a passing interest in wildlife cannot fail to be fascinated by the rich varieties of shore birds these inlets attract, particularly in winter, and the quality of light reflected and magnified by their still waters at sunrise and sunset is very special, and may be one of the reasons why painters like Walter Osborne and Nathaniel Hone had their summer retreats on the north County Dublin coast.

As I rounded the point, I was dismayed to see that the tide had risen faster than I had expected, and was covering the beach ahead. To continue, I had to clamber up a bank of rubble and building-site rubbish and, as I feared might happen at some stage of this coast-walk, I found myself in someone's garden. It was not a really formal garden, more a garden's end, the place where the grass cuttings and heaps of weeds are dumped, out of view of the house. Nearby, a man was cutting bushes with his back to me.

'Excuse me,' I called, 'I wonder would it be alright to get past there? I was walking along the shore and the tide caught me.'

The man turned. He was very elderly with a deep-lined face, and a kindly, if slightly bemused, smile.

'Come on, come on, you're alright. It's no bother,' he said, in a tremulous voice.

I apologised again, repeating that I had been caught by the tide.

'It's no problem, it's no problem at all. You could, of course, get by there if the tide was out, but if the tide is in, you can get stuck. You can come through here.' Taking me to a gap in the hedge between his garden and his neighbour's, he said, 'I can't give you permission. They're different people to me, you know, but once you go down there — ah, they won't see you — you can get to the sailing club.'

I told him I was heading for Portrane around the Rogerstown inlet, and I was hoping to cross the railway embankment.

'Well, you can go around to the railway and get on to the main road at Blakes Cross if you want, or cross by the railway, I suppose. But you just can't do it now without getting up on the headland. You see those trees and bushes?' He pointed a mile or so away westwards at the shore, but I could see no headland. 'You can walk all around because there's a big headland where the tractors go, and nobody'll stop ye. It's once you know the place, you know, you can get around by the strand, but you wouldn't get around now, you understand.'

I thanked him heartily for his advice. He waved farewell and returned to his gardening.

I passed by a tiny building which served as a clubhouse for the yacht club, and reached a track leading past Rogerstown Pier, where, a little offshore, a small fleet of yachts were straining at their moorings against a swiftly and noisily rising tide. Beyond the pier I passed a small, sea-battered harbour, around which a number of colourful fishing craft lay, propped up, awaiting repairs.

A tall, blond girl in her twenties came down a side road and walked alongside me. She said, 'Hello, isn't it a glorious day? Are you hiking?'

Pier at Rogerstown

I told her I was heading for Portrane and had been told to look for the 'headlands', which would take me in as far as the railway. 'I'm not sure what the "headlands" are,' I said. 'Are they cliffs of some sort?'

She told me that they were not really cliffs, but simply what the local people call the shore above the high-water-mark, and particularly the track that runs along there.

'Do you see the poles on the skyline?' she asked, pointing to the west. 'That's the Fingal dump; the railway runs immediately to this side of it. You should be able to cross under the tracks. What do you think of the area?'

I told her that what I had seen of it was very attractive, particularly the south beach.

'There are plans to develop a marina here, and the place needs work' — she pointed to the wrecked craft on the shore and the condition of the old pier — 'but it might never happen.'

We parted company, she going inland along a road called Sprout Road, while I continued along the shore road, the still-rising tide lapping at the stony edge. Soon, close to a tin-roofed cottage, the road dipped into the water of the inlet and disappeared. In the front garden of the cottage, like a nineteenth-century French painting of a rural scene, an elderly man and woman were sitting in the sunshine at a wooden table piled high with scallions. They were tying bunches of the vegetables and packing them in boxes. I wished them good afternoon, and asked them how to get on to the headlands. They directed me up a laneway beside the cottage, following a tractor that had just passed, loaded with boxes of flower bulbs.

The 'headlands' I had been puzzled about since my back-garden chat were exactly as the blond girl had explained — a track along the seaward side of extensive fields, from where, judging from clusters of startlingly pink gladioli surrounded by nettles and thistles in the hedge, a flower crop had recently been harvested. A

35

tractor was ploughing new drills, and a gang of teenagers was unloading boxes of bulbs from a trailer for the next crop. A ghetto-blaster on the trailer thumped out loud rock music as they worked. The sandy soils around Rush were famous in the eighteenth and nineteenth centuries for the early potatoes they produced, but in the 1890s much of the land was turned over, very successfully, to bulbs and flowers. I was sorry to have passed here just after harvesting; how amazing these fields must look when the crop is in full bloom.

I left the busy work and noisy music behind and came to a field where black-headed gulls, recently deprived by the tide of their foraging along the shore, were quartering the ground like swallows, catching flies and butterflies. Beyond them, on a rise in the ground, a mingled flock of more than a thousand oyster-catchers and gulls covered the middle of the field like some surrealist black-and-white crop. Even as I took in this wonderful scene, in one great flowing movement they launched into the air, squealing and piping at being disturbed at their siesta. As they gained height, the two species peeled off and separated into two great flying clouds, passing to either side of me like a shoal of fish avoiding a skin diver.

Looking through the hedge to my right, I could see that the tide was still creeping up the Rogerstown inlet, its tiny wavelets shepherding a line of straw, sticks and other flotsam on to the shore. Mullet, that large fish of shallow muddy inlets, were making their presence felt at the water's edge, leaping and splashing as they fed on newly inundated titbits. The almost calm waters were criss-crossed by the powerful bow-waves the bigger fish made as they sped along just below the surface.

Back towards the east, I saw that Lambay Island, sunless and ominous all morning, had finally come in range of the sun that was now bathing the countryside in warmth. To the west the vista was dominated by the Fingal dump, the garbage tip for most of north County Dublin. A tall fence of close-woven wire, decorated with a collage of plastic bags, topped an artificial hill towering above the railway embankment; the air was full of the roar of engines and clouds of dust as great bulldozers raced to keep pace with the deliveries of the ever-increasing garbage of a modern city. I descended to the shore and made my way over to the railway embankment, with not a little trepidation, because the tide was lapping against its base. If it were not possible to cross the embankment, I would have to walk a good distance further inland to cross the estuary and add nearly four miles to my day's journey.

The surprisingly steep embankment was clothed with a thick bed of brambles, so climbing it to the track was out of the question. I had no choice but to set out along the base of the embankment, a protective breakwater of large limestone boulders, around which the rising tide was now swirling. These boulders were unstable in places, but I made my way gingerly along, hoping to find some way up to the top before I reached the point where the railway was carried by viaduct over a place where the inlet narrowed to three hundred feet. I had to be sure-footed, striding and sometimes leaping from boulder to boulder, and I found that I was making slow progress. I also found it very tiring, so when I saw a patch where the brambles covering the slope had thinned out, I clambered to the top. Just as I poked my head over the lip at the level of the tracks, a train came hurtling by, making the ground tremble. I ducked down, and as soon as it had passed, climbed up, checking back along the way the train had come as I followed briskly in its wake.

The track stretched for a couple of miles into the distance like a lesson in perspective, and I soon got into the rhythm of walking on the concrete sleepers. The sun now was really beating down, and I knew I was beginning to burn; I promised myself either my remaining apple or drink when I had regained the shore on the other side. Arriving at the viaduct, I took a good look up and down the track, and crossed. The sea was racing under the viaduct into the western part of the inlet. A pair of shelduck shot over my head and swooped down to land on the water, joining a mixed flock of birds gathered to await the falling tide.

As I approached the embankment at the far side of the viaduct, I wondered if there were 'headlands' on the southern shore, and if I would find an easy way down off the railway. I was glad to spot a little pathway descending and, within a minute, after crossing a couple of strands of barbed wire, I was on the southern shore of the Rogerstown inlet. I had been led by my old 1870 one-inch map to believe that there would be a track or road here leading out to the burrows of Portrane, but there was none to be seen, and since the shore was too waterlogged to walk, I climbed a hedge bordering the shore and got into a field.

If it was warm up on the embankment, it was scorching down in the still, sheltered air of the high-hedged fields. The sun beat down on me, as if ridiculing my heavy rucksack, full of rain gear and warm clothing for the bad weather I had expected. I was perspiring profusely and beginning to feel dehydrated. The south-facing hedges, however, had an antidote — a marvellous crop of blackberries; after finishing my last apple and orange drink, I paused frequently to collect a handful of the fruit, popping juicy berries into my mouth like peanuts.

I came to a road that led me down on to the shore again, where I expected to find the old road to the Portrane burrows at a place called the Ramparts. There was none, however, but I did find a dry, meandering path through the salt marsh along the edge of the inlet. The glass calm of the full tide was disturbed along the shore by many mullet creating wavelets and splashes. They must be the only large seafish that can commonly be seen in great numbers, mainly because of their habit of feeding in shallow water; armed with a large net and waders I could have caught a lorry load that afternoon. Mullet are not popular with anglers because they live on decayed organic matter, and because their mouth parts are very tender and do not hold a fishing hook. With no natural enemies, they are a long-lived species, living for up to seventeen years and growing to as much as half a metre.

In addition to the usual rather dull plants commonly found, the salt marsh sported clumps of colourful sea aster, a wild flower like a daisy with a yellow centre and lilac petals, looking as if it had escaped from a garden. The ground became increasingly waterlogged as I progressed eastwards, and when I began to sink up to my ankles, I had to beat a retreat inland yet again and cross a ditch into the adjoining field. The field sloped up to the south, and at its highest point a ruined windmill stood, a robust cylinder of stone. A stone plaque over its door bore the date 1741 and the words 'Love God above all'. It is known locally as Carr's Mill, apparently after an eighteenth-century farmer who once owned it. I would not have thought that the Dublin coast was particularly renowned for its winds, but the remains of a number of these mills survive along the coast, three in the town of Skerries alone.

After a while, I was able to return to the shore. Crossing the ditch, I disturbed four herons, which squawked indignantly and rose in confusion on a rush of wings, like a scene from the African bush. It was almost three o'clock, and I was beginning to feel a little tired. The western side of Portrane burrows, a low-lying strip of yellow, dotted with a few houses and copses of trees, reflected perfectly on the glass-like surface of the inlet, and seemed to recede rather than get nearer. I kept close in to the hedge relishing its cool shade, and continuously disturbed rabbits, drowsing out of the heat of the sun.

Reaching a narrow but deep stream, I leapt across and soon after, with great relief, reached the end of the road that runs along the eastern side of the Burrow. Nearby was a hill called Knockmahon, only about twenty feet above sea level, but the highest point of the Burrow. Its name is probably derived from

Cnoc na mBan or the Hill of the Women, but up to a few decades ago it was a meeting place for local men, who on summer Sundays, in their dark suits and waistcoats, would gather to play cards and pitch and toss.

I walked inland along a laneway overhung with lilac bushes. The blackberries were no longer effective against my thirst, and I needed a drink of water. A dark-skinned oriental lady was sweeping outside a bungalow with her back to me, and when I called out to her over the wall to ask if there was a shop nearby, I gave her such a fright that she nearly fell over. When she regained her composure, she pointed back south towards Portrane and said there was one not far away. I had intended the query ostensibly as an opening to ask for a glass of water, but her fright and embarrassment sent her quickly indoors. I was not at this stage going to retrace my steps, so I licked my dry lips and walked on.

There were some beautiful houses set in their own grounds, and a few very old, long and low cottages along the roadside, but I saw no one else before I reached the end of the Burrow, and I could turn east and south again. As I reached the beach at the northernmost tip of the Burrow, it was strange to look across a mere hundred yards of water to the shore I had been walking on two hours before. A little further on, I met an elderly couple taking a short walk from their car parked nearby. I exchanged greetings and asked if they knew where I might get a drink of water. The man indicated a nearby caravan park, closed down for the winter, and told me there was a tap there to serve the caravans. I gave him a delighted thanks, and sure enough, within a few minutes, was thirstily enjoying a stream of cold and delicious water from a stand-pipe.

I felt a hundred times better now, and set off again with new heart.

Another opportunity to refresh myself came when I had to cross a shallow stream entering the sea from the marsh at the back of the beach; off came my boots and socks and I had a glorious paddle, lingering a while and squirming my toes on the sandy bottom. I left off my boots as I reached the main beach and set off southwards once more.

Lambay lay on an azure blue sea, now receiving the full afternoon sunshine, and white-washed cottages along its shore brightly reflected the light. The island is what remains of an ancient volcano; the craggy rock that makes up its northernmost point is called The Nose, but from where I was standing it looked more like the profile of a bearded face, gazing at the sky. A substantial wood above the harbour hides Lambay Castle, a beautiful and extensive country house designed in 1905 by Sir Edwin Lutyens on the site of a fifteenth-century castle. The house was built for the London banker Cecil Baring, who had bought the island a year or two before in response to an advertisement in *The Field* magazine announcing 'Irish Island for Sale'. Baring, who eventually became Lord Revelstoke, was the founder of Baring's Bank which collapsed in spectacular circumstances in 1994 when one of its junior traders in Singapore made eight hundred million pounds disappear into thin air.

Lambay is a fascinating island, and Baring was so interested in it that, between 1905 and 1906, he accommodated twenty naturalists from every branch of science while they carried out a thorough survey of its flora and fauna. The second Lord Revelstoke was concerned to preserve the island as a sanctuary for its animal and plant species, and in his later years was somewhat inconsistent in his attitude to visits, even from scholarly groups. In the 1970s a trip to the island by a group of eminent visiting geologists, arranged in advance by Trinity College, Dublin, was refused permission to land. Around the same time a yachtsman friend of mine landed at the little harbour without permission, was met by Revelstoke and invited up to the house for tea. At the time of writing, the second Lord Revelstoke has passed on, and an archaeological survey, the first ever undertaken on the island, is being carried out under the auspices of the Department of Archaeology, University College Dublin.

Ahead of me a dense flock of oyster-catchers was gathered at the water's edge, nervously flexing their wings at my approach. A massed piping began as a few birds at the perimeter of the flock took off, and then they were all airborne, in a pulsating mass of black and white plumage, accentuated by the low sunlight. Their wings made a whistling, rushing sound as they wheeled around, the flock becoming elongated as the leaders took it out across the sea and around to the now deserted point, before circling briefly and, almost as one, landing on the sands again.

I walked on to reach a fisherman who was tending his great bass rods near the edge of the surf. It had been he whom I had seen from Rush beach at lunch-time. As I drew up to him, he turned and gave me a twinkling smile as I remarked that he must have had a most relaxing day.

'Wasn't it a pet day! I've been here since about noon. I have a chalet there,' he gestured to the dunes behind the beach, 'and I came down, it was such a nice day. Just before you came along, I got my first bite of the day, on the other rod there, and struck, and the knot on the shot leader gave on me; one of those things. I was looking at it a half-an-hour ago saying I should replace this knot. It was a thumper of a bite, the only one I've got all day. I did get a little flounder and a few little dabs and things, but it was the only bass bite I got all day.'

'Is it a good place for bass?'

'Yeh. There's myself and about four other guys that have chalets here. You see them in the summer here with their wives and kids, but then they're all down here this time of the year for bass 'cause that's when the bass come in. But you need a bit of an easterly breeze, you know; you need a bit of surf.'

I asked him what he used for bait.

'Sand eels. There are two sand-eel bars out there — you can see where the tide is starting to ripple on them. We dig the eels there just before the tide rises.'

I told him that I had done some bass fishing years ago in Waterford, at a place called the Saleens.

'That's a famous place, still well known for bass. The numbers have dropped drastically in the past ten years, however, all over the country. This used to be a great place here. There was an old guy living in a chalet just back there,' he pointed into the dunes, 'it's burnt out now. We used to go out with him when we were kids of ten or twelve: get up at five in the morning, and be back in time for breakfast, always with a few fish. There's nothing like that now.'

He began to gather up his equipment.

'Wasn't it just a powerful day?' he said. 'I'll tell you: I thought when I woke this morning, it's going to rain, but I'll get a morning's fishing out of it. Well, about half two I rang some friends and suggested that they pick up some things in Marks and Spencers and come down and we'll have dinner here this evening.' He laughed at the idea of this spontaneous get together based on an unexpectedly warm day. 'One guy said I'm going to the gym and I said there's a lot of wet evenings ahead, come down and enjoy it! You see, that's my chalet there.'

He pointed to a beautifully restored, dark brown railway carriage a hundred feet back from the sea, parked on a grassy knoll. I admired it, saying I had spent a holiday in one as a child, and remember still the dark panelling, the brass trimmings, and the low curved ceilings.

'I repanelled it, put all the brass match-strikers back and all that; it's really good now. I mean you come down here at a weekend, you open the curtains in the morning to this view, right. And sitting out the back, you have the view over to Dublin Airport and the sunset. We have sunrise here,' he pointed towards

Lambay, 'and sunset on that side, over water. You have some wonderful evenings here. I live in central Dublin, and the reason I can live there is I have this here.'

'You certainly have things very well arranged,' I said enviously. He was justifiably proud of his *pied à terre*, and he asked as I moved off, 'Do you know what it cost me when I bought it? Eight hundred pounds.'

I gave the expected exclamation of disbelief.

'You know, you can't buy these carriages now. A few of them were brought down from Dublin in 1952, and that's the only one left. There was a beautiful double-decker tram here until about three months ago, but it was set on fire. About six months ago there was another railway carriage, and that was burnt as well. That's the only problem here — the vandalism is getting bad. I suppose there's always some problem!'

I wished him the best, and went on down the beach, leaving behind a man who had the art of relaxation well thought out: he had been standing and sitting on that sunny beach for four hours, with little to concern him other than the simple mechanics of fishing.

It was four o'clock now, and I was pleased that I was ahead of schedule, because I had only fifteen minutes walking to reach my destination, the old St Catherine's Church of Portrane. Ahead, the skyline of Portrane presented a strange assembly of silhouettes with its round tower, a beer glass-shaped, reinforced concrete water tower serving the hospital, a gothic clock tower and a tall brick chimney.

At the southern end of the beach I made my way inland a short distance to St Catherine's Church. I entered the churchyard through a squeaking gate, and walked around the roofless ruin, which is in good order for a structure that has seen over six hundred winters. As is the case with most churches of the period, the castellated tower served not only as a belfry, but as the priest's living accommodation. St Catherine's, originally dedicated to St Canice, is one of about sixty medieval churches, the remains of which survive in north County Dublin, an indication of the density of the population in the thirteenth century and the extent to which the church then dominated all aspects of life.

Eroded stone heads protruded from the masonry of the north and south walls of the church tower; I wondered if they were effigies of early incumbents, or images of St Canice. In spite of the thorough records kept by the disciplined Normans, the meanings of displayed carvings of heads such as these, and in some cases grotesque female figures called Sheila-na-gigs — graphically displaying their genitalia, on church buildings of this period is one of the many mysteries of their architecture. Another puzzle about this building and others of the same period is the slight and almost indiscernible batter or splay to the bottoms of tower walls, extending a metre or two from the ground. These refinements would have little or no effect in strengthening the walls, so are they purely an expensive and difficult-to-build visual feature?

Near St Catherine's Church, in the midst of a maze of semi-detached houses, are the battlemented remains of Portrane Castle, a thirteenth-century tower house. It is called locally Stella's Tower, after Dean Swift's paramour, Esther Johnson, who stayed there in 1712; the castle was last lived in around 1740, and presents a strange sight now, surrounded by Portrane's suburbia.

The name Portrane comes from Portrachrann, loosely translated as the harbour of Rechru, Rechru being the original name for Lambay Island. It is probable that this harbour stood at this sheltered end of Portrane beach, near St Catherine's Church. Although local tradition holds that the Danish kings of Dublin had 'summer palaces' in this area, it was off-the-beaten-track until its sleepy atmosphere was disturbed by the construction works on the Great Northern Railway line in the 1840s, which would have brought to the area a large and disruptive temporary population of engineers, surveyors and navvies. It had hardly drifted back into being a quiet backwater when, in 1896, it was chosen for the site of Ireland's biggest mental hospital, a development which was, at the time, the largest single building contract in Ireland. In the mid 1890s, a report of the Richmond District Health Board, which covered the Wicklow, Dublin and Louth areas, had recommended an extensive new hospital be established 'owing to a great increase in lunacy'. An architectural competition was held for the design of the hospital, and three vast schemes, with titles that today seem comic, 'Luna', 'Mens Sana' and 'Aspect', were short-listed, and the last-mentioned, by the architect George Ashlin, was chosen. Collen Brothers, the Dublin contractors, took on the contract, and overnight the area was inundated with building workers and tradesmen, many of whom were accommodated in temporary barracks near where the main entrance gates are today. The *Irish Builder* periodical reported in 1900 that 'where an architectural style is permissible the style adopted . . . is of a simple type of Tudor, which finds its finest expression in the chapels and dining hall.' The work continued until 1901, when the extensive redbrick complex, with its gothic pinnacles and clock tower, was completed, and the first of what was eventually to amount to twelve hundred patients were moved in.

I strolled down to the sea wall to daydream about royal Danish picnics and monks boarding a galley bound for Lambay, while awaiting my lift back to Dublin.

3

Portrane to Malahide

The weather forecast of the night before suggested strongly that rain was expected, so I was pleasantly surprised to set out on the next stage of my journey on a fine morning. It was a little cloudy, and a gusty wind scattered the sea with white horses, but I felt that, with luck, I would reach my destination, the town of Malahide, without getting too wet.

Portrane was quiet and there were few people about as I walked out along the shore from the beach and turned south to follow the coast past a row of flat-roofed coastguard cottages. The Irish Sea stretched east and south, gleaming in the early sun, and Lambay looked sombre and very different to the previous evening, when the setting sun had highlighted its western shores. Below the coastguard cottages on a rocky outcrop extending into the sea, a Martello tower, converted into a fine seaside villa, stood, surrounded by a richly planted, walled garden. Inland, Portrane's one-hundred-and-eighteen-foot round tower reached for the sky, easy to mistake at this distance, for an original medieval one. It is not the work, however, of the legendary Goban Saor, the magical builder who is reputed to have erected all the round towers of Ireland, and some of them in one night. This slender cylinder dates from 1844, when it was built for Sophia Evans of Portrane House as a memorial to her late husband, George.

The twisted volcanic rock formations and fantastic bubbles of stone along the cliffs south of Portrane, composed of an igneous cocktail of exotic-sounding minerals such as diorite, dolerite and andesite, look as if they have only recently been formed and pushed up out of the sea. We are fortunate that Portrane is one of those coastal places where the rich and descriptive names of every outcrop of rock and cave have survived, because they were collected and recorded in books such as the *History of Portrane and Donabate* written by Peadar Bates. As I walked, I looked out for features like the Chink Well, said to be a fresh water spring below the cliffs, and the Priest's Chamber, a hiding place for priests in penal times. I was disappointed, however, not to find these landmarks, nor one called the Bleeding Pig, a rock which apparently derives its name from its blood-like colour. I did, however, find a cave which I took to be the Piper's Hole, so named after the skeleton of a man was found there in 1844 near a corroded set of uilleann pipes. Into the same cave in the 1830s Sophia Evans brought a picnic party of ladies and gentlemen, and after they had penetrated deep under the cliffs, they enjoyed a meal of pigeon pie and champagne by lantern and torchlight. Their enjoyment turned to panic when it was discovered that the sea had risen and was entering the cave. It was all a Victorian entertainment, however, planned by Mrs Evans, and soon the guests were relieved to see a large boat being rowed into the cave to rescue them.

I came up to a group of five ragged men, three of them with skinny black greyhounds on leashes. Their dress and general appearance suggested that they were travelling people, and not of the somewhat better-off class that live in shiny aluminium caravans. They were poor itinerants, who probably slept in roadside tents, and very much resembled the tinkers I remembered from my childhood. Two of them were middle-aged, one with an unhealthy pallor and stained trousers a touch short, revealing that he had no socks in his down-at-heel shoes; the other was wearing a threadbare navy pinstripe suit over a dirty tee-shirt. The younger lads were more trendy and better dressed, in sweatshirts and jeans.

As I reached them, one of the older ones turned and said in a soft voice, which belied his rough and rakish appearance, 'Good mornin' boss! D'ye know are there any rabbits about here?'

I told him that I did not know the place well, but I

Latter-day Fianna

wouldn't be surprised if there were rabbits, and probably hares about, because hares were certainly plentiful a little further south along the coast. The mention of hares brought the interested attention of the rest of the group.

'Would there really be hares, would there?' the unhealthy one asked. 'That'd be good. I'd like to get a hare, but I'd settle for a rabbit.' He said this in such a way that I knew they were hunting not just for the sport, but for the food. They all looked as if they could do with a square meal. I asked him if they were hunting with the dogs, and he told me they were.

At the end of the wall we had been following along the shore bounding the grounds of St Ita's Hospital, we came to a low wire fence. The first man stopped and looked out over the broad field between the shore and the hospital. Suddenly he seemed to see something, and turning to me, said, 'Thank you, sir, good luck now!' and with a prodigious leap, cleared the fence. The others followed him, leading the dogs between the wires, and they all set out in a line abreast, across the broad expanse of cow pasture. At the far side of the field I spotted a further group of men with dogs, and realised that, with thirteen men and seven dogs quartering the field, this was an organised hunt.

Suddenly four of the dogs that had been straining at their leashes were released, to stretch out in long swift strides towards a quarry I could not see. Simultaneously, a roar of excitement went up from the hunters, and they too began to run in the wake of the dogs. The man nearest to me had not released his dog, but he was moving forward quickly, watching his companions streak ahead. Then he too unleashed his dog, which accelerated at an astonishing pace in a different direction, and at the same moment I saw, not too far away, a hare bound out of a clump of grass and shoot away, the hound at his heels.

A small herd of cattle that had been grazing quietly in the middle of the field now got involved in the excitement and began to run in an ungainly way after the men and dogs, kicking up clumps of turf as they went; and with whoops of delight, darting hither and thither after what were now apparently several hares, the whole circus disappeared around the high wall of St Ita's. For a long time after they had gone, I could still hear their excited shouts above the gentle sound of the sea.

It was as if I had come across a latter-day Fianna, warriors down on their luck, having lost their fine steeds and wolfhounds, reduced to hunting mere hares on foot. Indeed, I suppose I *had* met with the descendants of the Fianna, a few of the last real Celts. Their culture and circumstances made them reject the Sunday morning activities of modern man, with his sailboards, golf-clubs and footballs, and resort to the blood-stirring excitement of a hunt. I was reminded of a group of travellers I had come across near Ferbane, County Offaly a few years before. There was no resemblance between the unfortunate begging, drinking itinerant of the capital city and these people: three young families — the parents in their late twenties, the children all under ten. They glowed with health, the menfolk with thick black glossy hair and strong and sparkling white teeth, the women well-built and well-dressed beauties. Very much modern-day travellers, they had three good mobile homes, and what looked like an open-ended workshop on wheels, in which two of the men were carrying out repairs to a large generator. I had stopped to talk, and a little hutch beside one of the mobile homes caught my attention. In it was a fierce-looking, glossy-furred ferret, which they kept for hunting rabbits. Aerials on the caravan roofs showed that these families watched television; they obviously earned a living by doing complex mechanical repairs, but for their recreation, they resorted to a centuries-old hunting practice.

As I descended from the rocks on to a short stretch of beach, a straggling group of about fifteen female patients from St Ita's Hospital for the mentally handicapped came towards me, some of them holding hands with their carers, a trio of young nurses. The patients were dressed in garish clothing, mainly track suit bottoms and vinyl anoraks, and most of them were dragging their feet, shuffling forward as if coming to the end of a long and tiring journey. Some scurried to keep up, and one, her arms contorted into strange postures, gave a most distressing wail because she was being left behind. She was a small woman of indeterminate age with a head of fine silken blond hair, contrasting with her wrinkled and twisted features. Her hands and arms were frozen into the double-jointed postures of an oriental dancer. As I passed, not knowing how to help, one of the young nurses came back to rescue the tormented soul, who mercifully ceased her wailing as they all climbed up the beach and went through a gate into the hospital grounds.

Just before reaching Donabate beach I came across a little house, obviously someone's dream cottage, which had had lots of love and attention lavished upon it by its owner. Enriched with many decorative touches such as finials and shingles, the building overlooked a garden of shrubs and palm trees. Scattered about the garden were miniature pavilions and loggias, and in one corner, overlooking the sea, an entire and plainly original Georgian granite door case and arched entrance portico stood, presumably rescued from some old house under demolition.

As I walked on to Donabate beach past yet another Martello tower, I saw that the Dublin Mountains had a less distant look, and it was comforting to make out two new landmarks on the horizon: the vast Team Aer Lingus building at Dublin Airport and the high-rise tower blocks of Ballymun, indicating that I really was making progress towards the city and Dublin Bay. Ireland's Eye and Howth had assumed two separate sharp silhouettes, and in the hazy distance beyond the long, sandy beach, I could make out the outskirts of Malahide — white houses in serried ranks along the shore. A procession of wind-driven breakers was thundering on to the shore, and gusts of salt-laden air made the marram grass in the dunes at the back of the strand twist and wave in a terrestrial mimicry of the sea. The dune-system was under threat and heavy timber piles had been sunk along the front of the dunes to protect them from erosion. Coastal sand-dunes are a rich and rare habitat for flora and fauna, making up only two per cent of Ireland's land surface, but many such areas are under threat owing to the increasing numbers of people using beaches in summer-time.

Dunes like these were probably formed during post-glacial fluctuations, when the sea level changed from thirty metres lower than it is today to four metres higher, and then receded again to present levels. They provided Ireland's first mesolithic colonists with a safe, warm habitat; seafood, both fish and shellfish, wildfowl and wild fruit were even more plentiful than they are now, and the remains of their cooking activities — kitchen middens with abundant shells of cockles, oysters and mussels intermingled with burnt stones — are easily identified in dune areas.

In more recent centuries, after the Normans had introduced rabbits to Ireland, dunes like these at Donabate were found to be ideal for establishing rabbit warrens. With the sea surrounding three sides, it was a simple matter to fence the fourth side to keep the rabbits from escaping, and the owners of such places built up a substantial trade in rabbit skins and meat. Along the Dublin coast, names that include words like 'warren', 'coney' and 'burrow' have their origins in these endeavours. The industry declined only when escaped rabbits spread through the country, multiplying as only rabbits can and providing the populace with easy and fruitful hunting. During the late eighteenth century when the population of Ireland rose towards eight million, a new use was found for sand dunes and old rabbit warrens when every available piece of common land was put to use growing potatoes. Today most coastal dune areas provide for the very important need to drive little white balls long distances across grass and subsequently into holes in the ground.

The sand of the beach was firm to walk upon, and it was good to stride out, crunching razor- and mussel shells underfoot. In less than half an hour I was nearing the end of the beach; the town of Malahide seemed to be within a stone's throw. Flocks of ringed plovers mingled with sanderling at the water's edge, the latter scurrying along at such speed that their legs were a blur. Far out to sea there was an unusual sight, and I had to blink to ensure that what I was seeing was real; the sails and mast of an old-fashioned schooner making its way southwards were visible above the choppy waves. From where I stood the hull of the vessel was below the horizon, and that image, combined with the seeming antiquity of the vessel, gave the scene a ghostly feel.

I walked on around Malahide Point, from where the town's most dramatic recent development comes into view. Against the bulwark of a railway embankment that cuts across the Broadmeadow estuary, where substantial land has been claimed, a Mont St Michel of exclusive apartments was been completed. It dwarfs the town, and somehow its scale, design and the colouring of its towers and blocks make it look like a vast film set. The unreal quality of the scene was reinforced by a great flock of Brent geese grazing on the mud-flats before me. I mused that these graceful birds took no notice of how the surroundings of their feeding grounds were changing, and were just going about their instinctive way as their forebears had done since long before man had appeared in this part of the world. The first mesolithic colonists of these shores may have timed their wanderings along the east coast to coincide with the annual arrival of Brent flocks from Arctic Greenland, but obviously their predations did nothing to halt the migratory habits of the geese. Men equipped with firearms in more recent times must have decimated flocks, and posed a serious threat to the Brents' survival, but here they still were, sharing the world with man but taking little notice of him. A time may well come when man will have disappeared, but the geese will still arrive in autumn.

Brent geese

On my approach, the flock rose in a single flowing movement, and wheeled out over the inlet to settle a little way further on. In their midst I saw that a cormorant with an identity problem had happily but awkwardly kept his place.

Just a couple of hundred yards away a couple were strolling along the beach on the far side of the inlet. I now had about eight miles to walk before I would reach that point later in the day; so near and yet so far! The Malahide or Broadmeadow estuary is considerably greater than the Rogerstown inlet, a broad wilderness of saltings and mud-flats bisected by the north-south railway embankment. This time I decided not to follow the railway across to the south shore, but to go all the way inland until I could cross the first road-bridge over the Broadmeadow stream, a mile or so north of the town of Swords.

The distance I would have to walk to encircle the estuary was beginning to look daunting. Away in the distance stretched the northern shore, backed by rising ground, the rural skyline broken by a row of modern houses like a wagon train crossing a prairie; nearby was a thickly treed area marking the demesne of Newbridge House.

The tide was dropping swiftly now, exposing islands of seaweed which soon joined to become continents, landing grounds for many wildfowl which seemed to appear from nowhere to wheel, loop and alight. A chorus of plaintive squeals heralded a flock of lapwings which descended, flapping their clown-like wings, and landed close to where I was walking. Ignoring me, they immediately began to forage in the mud for the meal the tide had left behind.

I reached a tarmac road a little later, and passed a group of summer chalets sheltered by clumps of conifers. Some were quaint, old-fashioned and desirable holiday cottages on postage-stamp sites surrounded by hedges of escallonia. Others looked like mobile homes that had lost their mobility and taken root, their thin aluminium sides and roofs surreptitiously being replaced by bricks and felt, and their wheels magically turning into concrete block foundations.

As the road swung west again, I came to a gathering of old stables and cottages surrounded by trees and dominated by an old concrete grain silo. At the centre of the group was Corballis House, which is said to date back to Tudor times and is probably the oldest surviving house in the area. I was told that there are great oak floor beams in the house that came from a sailing ship wrecked on Portrane Strand.

The estuary shore ahead curved around towards the south and the railway embankment, but seemed to be mainly salt marsh and impenetrable scrub, so I decided to skirt around it. I followed the road under a railway bridge and reached the main Donabate road opposite the imposing gates to Newbridge House. This grand Georgian mansion of comfortable proportions was acquired by Fingal County Council in the 1980s and is open to the public.

Built in the late seventeenth century, Newbridge House has been the home of the Cobbe family for over two hundred and fifty years. In 1751 Thomas Cobbe married Elizabeth Beresford, daughter of the Earl of Tyrone, and she brought a dowry that was spent freely on remodelling the house and assembling a valuable art collection to adorn it. Their hospitality and their house parties were legendary; card playing was a particular favourite, and often games went on for two and three days, punctuated by much feasting. It was said of 'Old Tommie' Cobbe in the 1790s that he had not gone to bed sober in forty years. He was, I think, typical of that small clique of people who owned the greater part of Ireland throughout the eighteenth and the best part of the nineteenth centuries and who seem to have spent their time hunting, dining, drinking and gambling. I believe, however, that we are enjoying in many ways today the benefits of the far-seeing land husbandry of at least some of these landowners. Many of them were, in Yeats's words, 'no petty people'; the drainage of land and the clearing of scrub on a vast scale, and the planting of new woods of beech, chestnut and lime went some way towards replacing our lost oak woods, even if much of it was to provide themselves with good hunting country. Among the most outstanding legacies they have left are the fine houses they built in which to royally entertain their relations and friends, sometimes at a cost far beyond what their land holdings could bear, and often in competition with their equally spendthrift neighbours. Newbridge House is one of these.

Nearby, overlooking a tiny village green, complete with water pump, is the old church of Donabate, kept from ruination over the years mainly by the generosity of generations of Cobbes. When I wandered into the churchyard I was lucky to encounter Mick Farrell, the verger, a round-faced cherub of a man. I asked him about the place, and, enthused by my interest, he went over to his cottage to get his keys to allow me to see inside the church. While I waited, I wandered around the building, which seemed to have three distinct parts. The east end consisted of the remains of a castellated Norman tower, similar to that at Portrane, and probably dating from the thirteenth century. The middle bit could be sixteenth century, and there is evidence that the fine, curving, west gable is eighteenth century.

St Patrick's church Donabate

Mr Farrell arrived back with the keys and opened the heavy studded door. He led me through a tiny porch, where a seventeenth-century grave slab was mounted, and into the church. The new vicar was very go-ahead, he told me, and much of the church had been recently refurbished. The building had a comfortable, homely scale about it, but the gem of the interior was the little gallery erected for their own use by the Cobbe family. Its coved ceiling was a wonder of delicate, swirling Georgian plaster-work; the sanctuary area had been similarly plastered, Mr Farrell told me, but when the chancel was rebuilt in 1874, the old ceiling was not regarded as being in taste, and was demolished. A stained-glass window depicting The Raising of Lazarus was installed in the same year, a good example of the stained-glass of that period, but a poor substitute for the loss of a unique ceiling. Mr Farrell brought me down a couple of steps into the tiny vestry, the floor of which is almost entirely taken up by three great grave slabs dating from the early years of the eighteenth century.

'A woman was here with me one time. She came all the way from Canada, looking for her forebears,' he told me, 'and when she saw this, the middle headstone, she nearly went through the roof!' His voice echoed hollowly off the bare stone. 'Someone belonging to her was named on it, related to her mother. She nearly went hystoric altogether, unbelievable. "I found it, I found it!" she says. Her people were from Laytown somewhere, and when she seen that, the middle slab there, I was standing here, well, "Oh my God, I found it!" I made her day for her!'

We left the church, the big keys jangling as Mick Farrell pulled the great door shut with a deep thud. He pointed out a headstone in the graveyard and told me that Thomas Lewis Cobbe, the last of the male line of the family, had been buried there in 1984.

'His sister-in-law, that's his brother's wife, she's still alive, and her family, they're all in England. They can come home to the big house up above any time they want; there's a special place up there they can stay in — it's kept open for them. She was home here last Sunday; she was even here at church, and she caught me there at the gate. She came over and shook hands.'

Outside the gate, he stood with his hands on his hips.

'They were lovely people alright, a nice family. The last Mr Cobbe was a great cattle man, but if he got you on his land he'd shoot ye!'

'For trespassing?'

'Oh yeh, he would. He didn't want ye on his land at all, especially if ye had a dog. There's all game and everything like that on the land. I used to love wandering through the place, but one Sunday anyway as I rambled along he seen me; he was out counting cattle, an' he seen me, and I seen him, and I said I have no alternative but to face him. I'll go up to him anyway, and I didn't know what he was goin' to say. "Can you count?" he asked. "Be God," says I, "Mr Cobbe, I think I can."'

'He had this piece of paper in his hand, you see his herder never worked on a Sunday, "I'm after countin' them cattle out there," says he, "about ten times; there's supposed to be forty-two in it accordin' to this list, and I can only get forty."'

'"Well," says I, "Mr Cobbe, it's like this, count them a hundred times," says I, "and you'll still only get forty."'

'"What d'ye mean?" he asked, and I said, "There's two of them below just by the gate there, under the bushes, and to me, they're sick."'

'"Come on," he says, and up we go. And sure enough there they were. He saw quickly that they were sick, red water it was. "What am I going to do," he says, "How am I going to get them to the yard and all?" I says, "Would you not call Christy?" Christy was the herder, and he says, "He wouldn't work on a Sunday," so I says, "I'll give you a hand."'

'We got them to the yard anyway, and he says to me, "As long as you're alive, you have my permission to walk around my farm, any day or any time you want, but don't bring a dog with you," he says. He was a gentlemen.'

I shook Mr Farrell's hand and thanked him for letting me see the inside of the church; as I left, he was going through the gate into his cottage, chuckling at the memory of how he had made friends with the last Cobbe.

I retraced my steps and continued heading south-west once more, looking for an opportunity to cut down to the shore of the estuary. On the right of the narrow road, in an oval enclosure, stood the last remnant of the gable of Kilcrea church, one of the pre-Norman churches of this area, which became disused in the sixteenth century. Across the road from it, fronted by a pair of bushy lime trees, is Kilcrea House, a Georgian farmhouse with a good door case and venetian window. Before the railway embankment was built, the sea reached up a quarter-mile-wide inlet as far as here, and there used to be a little harbour close to the house. When the embankment was completed, the inlet began to silt up, and compensation had to be paid by the railway company for a mill that was put out of business. Today the inlet has disappeared and the land reclaimed.

The hedges on both sides of the road were hung down with great purple sloes, as big as small grapes, and I was amazed when I tasted them to find that they were almost as sweet. I had never seen sloes so big, nor tasted them so good; this crop was the result of the wonderful summer we had enjoyed. The old saying 'many sloes, many cold toes' suggests that plentiful sloes are the harbingers of cold winters, but I believe such things remind us of the past season rather than predict the future. The sloe is said to have many medicinal qualities, and country folk used to keep branches heavy with sloes hanging in the attic space, where the fruit dried slowly and was ready for instant use. An old English rhyme goes:

At the end of October go gathering sloes,
Have thou in readiness plenty of those
And keep them in bedstraw or still on the bough
To stay both the flux of thyself or thy cow.

The demesne wall of Seafield House lined the right-hand side of the road, and after a few minutes I came to the entrance gates. A yew and pampas-grass-lined avenue curved up to the house, which unfortunately was blocked from my view, but as a consolation I enjoyed the sight of a trio of grey squirrels playing tag in the grass, leaping and bounding after each other, until a black cat appeared, and they beat a retreat up the nearest tree.

I was relieved when the road led me back out to the Broadmeadow estuary again, along a demesne wall neatly topped with sea-rounded cobbles. A group of sailboarders were briskly preparing their boards for launching at the water's edge; one had already taken off across the water at speed, the brilliant colours of his sail startling against the grey-blue background of the sea.

The narrow road continued as a track between the demesne wall and the sea, and at a damaged section of wall I was able to stand on tiptoe and get a glimpse of Seafield House, which at the time was the home of Sir Robert and Lady Goff. It is a palatial building with a very impressive entrance, twelve broad steps leading up to the entrance door under a six-metre-high classical portico supported by four doric columns. The elevational features of the house, particularly the low second-storey windows and the proportions of the first-floor windows, suggest that it might be the work of Leinster House architect Richard Castle, who is also thought to have prepared designs for nearby Newbridge House. The portico was probably added, together with the west wing and its Italianate tower in the halcyon days of the nineteenth century. In 1892 Seafield had been considered for the siting of the lunatic asylum that was eventually established at Portrane; at the time the asking price was thirteen thousand pounds. A few months after I passed by, this great house and its demesne were sold to a British businessman for over a million pounds.

The track soon became a narrow margin between the sea and the wall, but because the tide was going out, it looked as if I was not in danger of getting wet if I continued on. Looking back, I could see the dunes of Portrane a couple of miles to the east, over the top of the long railway embankment, while to the west was the unmistakable silhouette of the round tower in the town of Swords. It seems possible that in early Christian times the Broadmeadow estuary was navigable to ocean-going ships, and although the town of Swords is today regarded as an inland place, the monastic settlement there may have had easy access to the sea at that time. This advantage subsequently became the establishment's downfall, and Swords was probably one of the first of the Irish monasteries to be pillaged and burned by Viking raiders.

As the shore of the inlet turned towards the south, I reached a grove of beech trees in which a house nestled cosily, surrounded by substantial stone walls. The walls had a batter to them and looked as if they had once surrounded something considerably more important. Nearby, an ancient bridge spanned a river that drained into the estuary, and with tiny wavelets lapping at the shore, the scene resembled a Constable painting.

Cormorant

Although the tide was going out, I found that the track I was following was still covered by the receding sea for a couple of hundred yards, so I had to clamber up on to the sea wall until the track reappeared. The estuary was becoming narrower as I proceeded, and it was clear that there was little depth of water now; fifty yards from the shore a cormorant perched, hanging its wings out to dry, on the top of an almost-submerged supermarket trolley.

The afternoon had been darkened by a bank of grey clouds that had shifted in from the west on the wind, and it was getting chilly. I followed a blackthorn-screened stone wall, bordering the demesne of Lissenhall, another very old property surrounded by holm oaks. The estuary was scattered with islands and mud-flats, all occupied by flocks of birds, the most numerous being oyster-catchers, standing like a convention of head waiters, facing into the wind. I came upon a wedge of swans, thirty at least, gathered around a parked car, the air above them filled with jinking black-headed gulls. It was an astonishing sight. In the car a young girl was helping her father feed the swans with bread through the car window, lowered an inch for the purpose. Swans stood patiently at the opposite window, comically peering into the car and awaiting their turn to be fed. They all had identifying rings around their ankles and were extraordinarily tame, approaching me when I came along, although they came no closer than a couple of yards. A sign near the shore indicated that the area was a swans' sanctuary, and another said 'SOS — Save our Wildlife — No Motorway Here!' Further on I noticed that the overhead telegraph wires were hung with strips of colourful plastic, presumably to make the wire more visible to swans in flight.

The estuary now narrowed to become the Broadmeadow Water, a swift-flowing stream, and I sat on its banks to eat a sandwich. The water was not very deep, and as I ate I began to notice the collection of litter on the bottom. A tree branch that resembled a female leg daintily pointed its foot at the surface like some abandoned underwater combination dancer. A supermarket trolley was ending its days lodged on the bottom, netting all kinds of dreadful things from the fast-flowing water. An old, still-padlocked travelling trunk that looked as if it might contain treasure was protected by a condom that had become attached to one of its clasps, and which was being held ridiculously erect by the current. It was not a very appetising scene, so I left and finished my sandwich on foot.

A short distance further on I finally crossed the Broadmeadow Water by the narrow Lissenhall Bridge, and in minutes was heading eastwards towards the sea again. I passed a junction called Seatown Road further on, but of Seatown Castle, shown on my old map, I could find no trace.

Dublin County Council has established a linear park along this stretch of the Broadmeadow inlet from Lissenhall to Malahide, a useful amenity that would be hugely improved by the planting of a hedge separating the grassy banks and footpath from the road. This is a good place for bird-watchers to see a rich variety of water-fowl and waders. The tide was turning, and formations of birds of all kinds were alighting on the shallow waters. Although I soon lost count of the species I could not identify, I recognised great crested grebes, widgeon and mergansers in little groups bobbing about just offshore, busily diving for food. In the general peacefulness of it all, I got quite a fright when I disturbed a great, grey heron that had been standing at the water's edge, and he rose with a loud, raucous squawk to let the wind take him further east.

I turned inland briefly at the Malahide Sailing Club to pass through an area called The Yellow Walls in the richly treed outskirts of the town. The strange name is a throw-back to the seventh century, when the place was used as a drying green, and the walls became stained yellow from the dyes in the linens that had been draped over them to dry.

I reached the shore again near a sailboard club, and the massive new 'condo' development that I had first seen from the other side that morning came into view ahead, a series of urban cliff faces of balconied apartments. Minutes later, I passed under the railway embankment into the middle of the bustling and prosperous dormitory town of Malahide.

Sea-margined Malahide must be a pleasant and healthy place in which to live; there is evidence that this was among the places on the east coast in which Ireland's earliest inhabitants, a mesolithic tribe, called by archaeologists the Sandelian people, settled nearly nine thousand years ago. The name comes from

Mount Sandel on the river Bann south of Coleraine, where evidence of thousands of years of occupation by early man has been carefully excavated by archaeologists, including the camp sites of the earliest people to live in Ireland. Tiny flint tools called microliths, similar to those used by Mount Sandel people, have also been found near Malahide, suggesting that some of them came south, or that more of the colonisers came directly west from Britain. They might have used the partial land-bridge that some archaeologists suggest still existed at the time, crossing channels between drumlin islands in dug-out canoes.

There is evidence that a millennium later another race, known as the Larnians, also enjoyed the sea air at Malahide. Although the Larnians did clear small areas of the forest for agricultural purposes, both they and the Sandelians lived primarily on hunting small game and catching fish, in addition to collecting shellfish and nuts and fruit. My day on the perimeter of the Broadmeadow estuary had shown that both these prehistoric tribes could live well in the area today.

Later in time, according to legend, another people came and settled at Malahide. They were called the Firdomhnainn, the Children of the Goddess Danu, and were said to be a race of magicians and sorcerers who subsequently played a major part in the mythology of Ireland. They gave Malahide its first name — Inver-Domnainn, or the river-mouth of the Danannans.

A thousand years ago the Scandinavian seafarers found the sheltered Broadmeadow estuary a safe place for wintering their ships, and eventually a permanent settlement developed on the shore. They were quick to see the potential of the tidal race out through the narrow sound, because they are known to have constructed and operated a tidal mill there, probably the first of its kind to be seen in Ireland. More such mills were built along the shore in subsequent centuries, and the technology was still in use over six hundred years later when the Petty Survey noted that 'there are . . . many thatched houses and cabins by the seaside or bay, where fishermen dwelleth, and a mill that goeth by ebb tides'.

Viking control of Malahide ceased only when the Normans began to take control of Ireland's east coast in 1170. Richard Talbot, one of the Norman knights who accompanied Henry II to Ireland, received a grant of the territories surrounding Malahide in 1185 and, as was common at the time, established a motte and bailey on the higher ground above the seashore from which he began to organise and develop his land. Around A.D. 1200 a stone castle was erected, and over subsequent centuries many alterations and additions were carried out. The Talbot family occupied Malahide Castle up to 1973, nearly eight hundred years, which must be a record in Ireland, and the castle, now open to the public, contains a rich collection of historical memorabilia.

4

Malahide to Howth

The people of Malahide have an excellent amenity in the promenade pathway that winds out from the town along the coast and around the corner to Portmarnock. Summer or winter, it is a great place to stretch your legs and let the sea breezes blow in your face, with the sound of the sea on rocks and sand, and the calls of the gulls filling the air.

I followed the path uphill out of Malahide as it wound eastwards. I passed a Martello tower, known locally as Pa Hicks's Tower after Frederick Hicks, the owner and architect who was responsible in 1911 for its excellent conversion into a dwelling. Its battered walls were clothed in Virginia creeper, and this, combined with a generous and steep ochre-tiled conical roof with dormer windows, gave the building a fairy-tale look. Conversions of Martello towers have been tried many times, yet one rarely comes across a case such as this where the owner has blended sufficient money and sensitivity to achieve success.

Pa Hicks's Tower

Further on I passed a fifteenth-century tower house called Robswall Castle, built to oversee shipping entering the Broadmeadow estuary. In the early sixteenth century it and the lands and seashore about were leased by Cistercian monks from the powerful St Mary's Abbey of Dublin, and they built up a considerable monastery around the castle. They collected a feudal tax of six hundred fish a year from the local fisher-folk, and sought and were granted entitlement to all the flotsam and jetsam washed up on this part of the coast, including wrecks. In those days of primitive sail, this was often a valuable right.

From Robswall Castle I could see back a long way north once more, to the Rockabills lighthouse reflecting in the morning sun, while to the south-east, rugged Ireland's Eye stood off Howth. The buildings of the town were now visible, stepping up towards the summit of the headland.

As the shore swept around to the south, another Martello tower came into view and beyond it the broad and surf-fringed sands of Portmarnock, the Velvet Strand, stretched into the bright distance. Past the southern tip of the strand I could see the narrow and low-lying strip of land at Sutton which linked the mass of Howth to the mainland. Before descending to the beach, I went into one of the shops overlooking the sea to get some fruit. The proprietor was standing at the door gazing intently out to sea through a pair of binoculars; it struck me that there must be few shops in the country with such an outlook, and through the seasons it would be difficult not to take a keen interest in the sea and all the craft that passed by. I bought a few bananas, crossed the road to the strand and struck out for the far end, almost two miles away.

This uninterrupted length of firm flat sands were used by the Australian flyer Charles Kingsford Smith and his companions as the take-off point for their attempt to complete the first east-to-west flight of the Atlantic in June 1930. Kingsford Smith had arrived in Ireland earlier that month with a co-pilot and engineer in a Fokker monoplane, named the *Southern Cross*. They were in need of a navigator for the flight, and an advertisement placed in

The Irish Times seeking one for the Atlantic flight attracted a huge response, although few applicants had any qualifications or experience for the job. Captain Paddy Saul, son of a Dublin coal merchant, was quickly accepted. He had an interesting background. He had 'gone to sea' as a young man, and had rounded Cape Horn three times before his twentieth birthday! During World War I, he had served with the Royal Engineers but afterwards he went back to the sea. Paddy Saul had become interested in aviation during the war, however, and he soon returned to Ireland where he became involved with the newly formed Irish Aero Club.

The Irish Army Air Corps had begun lengthening the runway at the Curragh Camp so that the big aircraft, heavily laden with fuel, could get off the ground, but the aviators became impatient to leave while the weather was good. On hearing of the firm, smooth sands of Portmarnock, Kingsford Smith came to see the beach for himself and immediately made a change of plan. The pioneering and dangerous attempt to cross the Atlantic to New York would begin here.

After spending the night of 23 June in the Grand Hotel in Malahide, the flyers climbed on board the aircraft, which had been flown from Baldonnel the day before, and, in spite of warnings of poor weather from the far side of the Atlantic, they took off at dawn, cheered on by a huge crowd, many of whom had waited all night to see the take-off. Thirty hours later, in conditions of poor visibility, they had had to abandon the attempt to get as far as New York, but succeeded in crossing the Atlantic from east to west when they landed in Newfoundland. Like many of the other aerial pioneers of the period, Kingsford Smith disappeared five years later while on a flight over the Bay of Bengal, but the original *Southern Cross* was preserved and is on display today in a museum near Brisbane, Australia.

Irish aviation enthusiasts again crowded to Portmarnock two

years later when Jim Mollison, aviator husband of Amelia Earhart, took off in a De Havilland Puss Moth to attempt the first single-handed flight of the Atlantic, east to west. After a difficult flight of thirty-one hours into strong headwinds, he too succeeded in reaching Newfoundland.

The Velvet Strand's popularity as a leisure amenity was borne out by the large numbers of people stretching their legs on its spacious sands. Fathers played football with their children, dogs ran to their hearts' content, joggers jogged, and three men, well apart from each other, were treasure-hunting on the sands using metal detectors. I approached one of them, a bearded man in a German army surplus coat, who was trawling along at the water's edge, being harried by a little dog who kept up a rhythmic barking. I asked him if he had found anything interesting. He lifted earphones from his ears to hear me and, in a Northern accent, said that the beach level had increased in recent storms, bringing up things that had been buried for a long time. I asked him what kinds of finds were common here, and he told me that over a long period of time he had found quite a lot of gold rings. 'None today, unfortunately,' he said. 'They usually lie in the black sand which gets thrown up from time to time. Two weeks ago I was down here and got a ring, gold cuff-links dated 1899, and a sixteenth-century silver spoon, but there would be days when you would try for hours and get nothing.'

I marvelled at this as I left him; whatever about the ring and cuff-links, the spoon would have a tale to tell. There is a certain magic in this technology that allows one to find a veritable needle in a haystack.

The dunes to my right were becoming higher, but elaborate breakwaters strung along them showed that they were periodically under threat. The light, sandy soil of the Portmarnock dunes has a rich flora that includes over two hundred and fifty different species of plant, some of them quite rare. The fascinating Bee

Orchid, with each flower looking as if it has a bee climbing into it for nectar, can be found in the grasslands behind the beach, as can Spotted Orchids and the Hairy Violet, one of Ireland's endangered plants.

Ahead of me a woman and a man were bent over looking intently at something on the ground. When I came up to them, I saw that the woman was photographing a scattering of razor-shells and flotsam. There were enormous numbers of razor-shells on the beach, both the big straight ones and the smaller, finer curved type, as well as mussel and otter shells. There were also many whelks, and when I lifted one from the sand, I was surprised to find that it still contained its owner, albeit no longer alive. Intermingled with the shells were many knobbly chunks of what could have only been a variety of sponge, again something I had not seen before on an Irish shore. It was good to note that there was little or no rubbish on the beach and none of the ubiquitous plastic bottles one might expect so close to Dublin.

Towards the southern point of the strand the dunes were much less tall; the last one-sixth of a mile of the peninsula has since 1900 materialised out of the sea, allowing the Portmarnock Golf Club, which occupies the interior of the sand-duned peninsula, to expand southwards. Near the point, there were great numbers of sea-birds vigorously feeding at the edge of the tide, and they took off in a cloud, calling indignantly at my approach.

I crossed into the grassy interior to reach the western shore of the peninsula, passing a small man-made lake, fringed with reeds and designed to be part of the extended golf course. The far shore of the inlet came into view as I reached the water again, with the convent, seminary and church of Baldoyle forming a dense cluster of high buildings. As I made my way north, the buildings of Portmarnock Golf Club, topped by a tricolour, came into view.

A lone golfer, carrying his clubs in a bag slung from his shoulder, came over a rise, reached a tee-off point, set down his bag and prepared to drive. I stopped to watch. He paused carefully, took a trial swing, and then, moving into the ball, swung slowly back and drove, the golf-club connecting with the ball with a satisfying 'thuck', sending it hissing away across the course. Only when the golfer moved off did I realise that a large flock of Brent geese was grazing nearby, taking no notice whatever of the movement or noise.

A golf buggy came over the rise, a bulky man in a cap driving and a collie dog sitting up on the seat beside him. Whether it was the vehicle or the dog was not clear, but one or both disturbed the geese, and they took off in unison, calling loudly, and swept away in a beautiful flowing motion. There is something fascinating about the flight of a large flock of these birds — the military precision and the unison of their formations is marvellous to behold.

The golf club buildings were extensive and palatial, with a red clay-tiled roof and copper-domed clock tower. Golf is a game that seems to inspire great passion, irrespective of the level of its proponents' play. It was a Scottish invention, and the first Irish course was established on the Curragh of Kildare by a Scot, David Richie, in 1852. Interest in 'Scottish Golf' spread quickly, initially among the Scottish community in Ireland, members of which were responsible for the establishment of most of the original clubs. Two such Scotsmen, W.C. Pickman and George Ross, established the course at Portmarnock, and the club was founded in 1893. The enthusiasm of the early players here was such that, rather than waste time travelling the three miles around from Sutton by road, horse-drawn charabancs were availed of to cross directly at low tide.

As I passed near the clubhouse, a little wary in case I was trespassing, the golf cart I had seen earlier pulled up nearby, and the driver, leaving the dog sitting there, came across to me.

'Good morning,' he said courteously. 'I hope you are not taking photographs of the course. I'm afraid it isn't allowed.'

I replied that I was photographing the coast and wildlife. He was obviously a keen naturalist, because in minutes he was telling me about the rich fauna that inhabited the peninsula, and how the club were taking good care that it remained like that. He said that among the birds nesting in the area are barn owls, sometimes short-eared owls, sparrow hawks and kestrels, and that cuckoos were common in May.

'Did you ever get a shot of a cuckoo?' he asked. 'You would have no trouble here — there are plenty of opportunities; a pair of them come every year.' He told me that he had recently bought a video camera, and one of the first scenes he had filmed involved a spectacular fight between a grey-backed crow and a hare near his cottage on the grounds. He pointed out across the inlet and told me about the flocks of knots, tiny wading birds, that congregate in great numbers on the mud-flats.

'When there's a thousand or so of the birds flying together, it is a marvellous sight. If you carry on along here, there's a possibility that you'll see them and get a few good pictures.'

I thanked him and walked on along the edge of the practice course towards the dormitory town of Portmarnock where row upon row of triangular gables seemed to march into the distance. I watched a lone man out on the mud banks vigorously digging for lugworms. The sunlight played with many shades of violet on the calm waters of the inlet, and indeed, before long, a great flock of knots took to the air ahead of me, their silvery underparts flashing as they wheeled and turned. The knot is another species of migrant bird that finds the Dublin coast a good place to visit while Iceland, Greenland and northern Canada, their home for the rest of the year, are deep in winter. Their flocks have been known to number as many as ten thousand birds, but even in much smaller groups their marvellous formation aerobatics are a spectacular sight.

Since I had passed Portrane, I had been conscious of the constant procession of aircraft descending to land at Dublin Airport. Here at Portmarnock, however, the flight path for their final approach was directly overhead, and planes of all colours and shapes were thundering over and dropping their wheels, at a rate of one every eight minutes. They were so loud and low, one was tempted to duck each time.

To get to the mainland again, I had to skirt the mud-flats at the top of the Baldoyle inlet by cutting through a corner of Portmarnock's suburbia to reach the main road. Looking back towards the town, I saw that I had missed such epicurean and gourmet delights as Mr Gandhi's Tandoori Take-Away, The Wooden Spoon and the Sea Palace Chinese Restaurant. On the road I quickened my pace; I had almost another four miles left to walk before I would reach Howth and I was hoping to make it by way of the seashore for most of the distance if it was possible to do so. But the tide was imperceptibly rising, and I really did not know how far I would get before I would have to turn inland.

After a few minutes I left Portmarnock behind and followed the road around to the western side of the Baldoyle inlet. To the east now a broad reed-bed called the Murrough extended, while to the west stretched acre upon rolling acre of furrowed fields, their early sprouting crops a mist of pale green across their surfaces. I crossed a bridge over the outlet of the Maine river, stopping on my way to admire the flocks of long-legged waders grazing the nourishment-rich mud-flats below. The Maine and its tributary,

the Cuckoo, used to drain the
lands of Collinstown to the
west, and today continue much
of their age-old courses in
culverts beneath the airport
runways.

Sanderling

Beyond the river I came to
the blocked up gateway to the
disused Baldoyle Racecourse,
which closed in the 1970s.
The third Earl of Howth had
established it in 1860, and it was the first course in Ireland to be
fully enclosed. Before this time, race meetings were held 'cross-
country' or on suitable beaches such as Laytown in County Meath
or Tramore in County Waterford. The Baldoyle course was
particularly successful because, owing to its early establishment, it
was able to claim the best dates for its fixtures, such as New Year's
Day and St Patrick's Day, and its proximity to Dublin and the
existence of the railway always ensured large crowds of punters.
When I passed by, the old racecourse, like so many other tracts of
flat land on the outskirts of the capital city, silently awaited
development for housing behind anonymous walls that gave no
hint of the place's former glory.

After passing a pair of neat cottages occupying a cultivated
oasis in the midst of the marsh, I descended to the shore, relieved
to leave behind the busy road. Two vessels lay leaning on the stony
shore, one a speedboat, the other a more substantial cruiser. They
reminded me of old photographs of Baldoyle depicting fishing
boats drawn up on the shore; local people still talk of an old man
who lived in one such hulk for some twenty years at the end of the
nineteenth century. Scattered along the imperceptibly rising tide
beyond the two boats were a great number of Brent geese, a most
attractive and peaceful scene. The glassy calm of the inlet provided

a perfect reflection of the far shore with its terracotta-roofed golf club set amidst a grove of dark conifers. Beyond the dunes and behind the club the rugged summit of Ireland's Eye caught the sun.

The stony shore was comfortable to walk upon, and I soon found myself beneath the tall gables of Baldoyle church, which is perched right at the edge of the sea wall. It is the tallest and most significant building in the area, and must have been an impressive sight when it was built in 1831; at the time Baldoyle consisted of a gathering of fishermen's *bothans* along the shore, and an inn, which is depicted by William Sadler (1792–1839) in a painting in the National Gallery of Ireland. In common with many of the east coast inlets, the place was formerly a Scandinavian trading post; the name Baldoyle derives from *Baile Dubh Gall*, or the town of the dark stranger.

The shore at Baldoyle

Baldoyle church, one of the earliest substantial Catholic churches to be erected on a street-front site after the repeal of the Penal Laws, was built to replace a former thatched structure, some remains of which still lie undisturbed below the floor of the present building. It is a simple but dignified building, the only external decoration being its Lambay granite pilastered and pedimented entrance elevation. The only out-of-place feature is its copper-clad bellcote; under the roof, a substantial structure exists which suggests that a more elaborate spire or tower was originally intended, but a lack of funds must have prevented this from being realised.

Beyond Baldoyle village, the shore began to curve around towards the sea and another sand-duned spit of land extending north towards Portmarnock beach called Cush Point. At this point, Dublin Bay was only a few hundred yards to my right, across the neck of low land that joins the promontory of Howth to the mainland. Sutton Golf Club occupied Cush Point, and I skirted inland around it until I was able to turn down to the shore and enjoy walking on sand again. Beyond the eastern end of the beach, a promontory of boulder clay topped by a copse of Scots pines, I could see Howth Harbour not far away. I asked a man walking his dog if I would make it around to Howth before the tide would cut me off, and he indicated that I would.

I carried on briskly, but when I got to the promontory, the waves were lapping at its steep rocky base. There was no way of knowing whether the tide was in or not on the far side of the promontory, other than by making my way around, so I quickly took off my boots and socks, and, rolling up my trousers, stepped into the water. By the time I was five yards into the sea and it was lapping about my knees, the surprising coldness of the water hit me. An excruciating pain enveloped my feet, and rather than easing away in moments as I acclimatised to the temperature, it steadily increased in intensity. Since I still could not see how much further I would have to paddle, and because I could stand the cold no longer, I hobbled woefully back to the beach and stumbled around in agony, slapping my feet on the sand to speed up the circulation. After a pause, I tried again, but was driven back once more. These two defeats took away all my resolve and, quickly making excuses for myself, I gave up, deciding to go around the promontory inland. So, having returned my shocked feet to their gloriously warm socks and boots, I retraced my tingling steps a short distance and reached the road again.

The road led me down a cul-de-sac, at the end of which a sign warned me not to trespass into a small demesne that had been divided into three parcels of pleasant wooded gardens, each with its secluded house. To the right of the entrance gate, however, was an almost imperceptible pathway through shrubs, and I found it bypassed the demesne along a narrow silvan corridor bounded on the other side by the DART line. This led me out into the open again and into the grounds of a hotel adjoining the beach. A wall separated the hotel grounds from the beach, and there seemed to be no access other than through a gate, which I found to be locked. I was growing a little weary now, and did not relish the idea of backtracking yet again, so I asked a young barman carrying a crate of beer if there was any way to get on to the beach. This saviour took some keys from his pocket and, leading me to the padlocked gate, opened it and let me out.

My weariness subsided when I saw that I had only a short distance to go, and in a few minutes I ascended beside the DART station and, passing through a narrow alley, found myself walking the harbour of Howth.

The earliest known historical reference to Howth is on a map prepared in the second century by the Alexandrian Ptolemy, the most important geographer of his time. Although the period boasted a number of brilliant mathematicians and astronomers, Ptolemy is probably best known because much of his work survived. On his map of western Europe, Howth is shown as an island called Edri Deserta, meaning the deserted place of Edar, an ancient name of Howth, referring to a chieftain of the *Tuatha de Danann* who is said to be buried on the summit. Although Ptolemy never visited most of the places he depicted, his maps are remarkably accurate for the time, and the fact that Howth is shown as an island suggests that the narrow isthmus of Sutton, which joins the promontory to the mainland, did not exist nineteen hundred years ago.

The name Howth is derived from a old Scandinavian word for head; the sheltered northern shore of the promontory was used by the Scandinavians in the ninth century, initially as a wintering base, but a sizeable settlement must have existed when Sitric, King of Norse Dublin, established a church there in 1042. In the twelfth century the Normans, led by a knight named Sir Almeric, ousted the Howth Scandinavians at the battle of Evora Bridge, which spanned a little stream close to where the DART station is today. During the building of the station in the nineteenth century it is said that bones and armour, possibly dating back to this battle, were found. The battle took place on the feast-day of St Lawrence, and the Norman victor took that name in thanksgiving when he was granted Howth and other lands for his prowess in battle. In the thirteenth century the old church was replaced by St Mary's Abbey, which served for three hundred years until Henry VIII's time. For the succeeding two hundred years before the coming of the harbour and later the railway, Howth was wild and little inhabited; with the exception of Howth Castle, the home of the St Lawrence family, the only dwellings were a cluster of miserable hovels on the shore, belonging to poor fisher-folk.

In the early nineteenth century Howth competed with Kingstown for the establishment of a packet station to replace the Pigeon House, and the relative merits of both places were fiercely contested by the respective land-owners. A contemporary pro-Kingstown pamphleteer indicated the uninhabited 'badlands' nature of the Sutton area at that time when he pointed out that a troop of horses would be needed, and a gunboat offshore, to prevent the mail coach from being plundered by pirates or highwaymen on the Howth road.

The land-owners of the Howth area, however, won the day. The construction of the new harbour, supervised by the Scotsman

John Rennie, enclosing a safe anchorage fifty-two acres in area, began in 1807. The science of hydraulics was not well understood at the time, however, and in common with other harbours built around Ireland during that period, the new harbour, completed for a remarkably high cost for the time of three hundred thousand pounds, silted up within a year. By 1820 it had become clear that it would not be practical to keep the harbour dredged to accept the packet boat, and within a few years the station had been removed to Kingstown.

Every cloud has a silver lining, however, and before long the harbour became a major base during the summer months for a fleet of herring fishing boats from all parts of Ireland, Scotland, Wales and England. On the arrival of the railway in 1844 and, with it, the era of annual holidays, Howth became a popular watering place for Dubliners. Howth is no longer miserable, and it would be difficult to find a hovel there today; houses on its hilly coast, overlooking a view as fine as that of the Bay of Naples, are among the most expensive in Ireland.

5

Howth to Sutton

On a dull morning I started out from Howth Harbour to circle the promontory, which I reckoned would give me my last taste of rural County Dublin, because from Sutton to the Wicklow border, the shore is mostly man-made and the hinterland built up. My plan for the day was to follow the coastal cliff path around Howth Head to reach the low-lying Sutton coast, and then follow the shore towards Clontarf, a distance of about twelve miles.

A sharp breeze raised a cacophonic rattling of ropes against the waving forest of aluminium masts beyond the blue-and-white-striped Howth Yacht Club. Beshoff's fish and chip shop on the pier was closed, and nearby, a night-club called Good Time Charlies looked forlorn in the pale morning light. There was little sign of life.

I walked towards the crescent of tall buildings that overlooks the harbour. Behind, the skyline was dominated by the gaunt ruins of St Mary's Abbey, built during the fourteenth and fifteenth centuries. The triple belfry on its west gable once held three bells which, it is said, could be heard as far away as Lusk, ten miles to the north; in foggy weather the bells were rung to guide Howth's fishermen back to harbour. In the Abbey you will find two fine fifteenth-century tombs adorned with richly carved effigies, commemorating Sir Christopher St Lawrence, thirteenth Baron of Howth, and his wife, Anna Plunkett.

I passed the Portofino Restaurant, the Fisherman's Bar and a brief rash of modern balconied apartments, in the midst of which the granite-faced, bow-gabled and finely proportioned Howth House looked disdainfully dignified. It was built in the early 1800s for Captain George Taylor, the engineer who oversaw the construction of the harbour, and for many years was the only house on this shore.

The east pier is where most of the guns used in the Easter Rebellion of 1916 were landed in broad daylight in July 1914. A shipment of fifteen hundred rifles and fifty thousand rounds of ammunition had been bought in Germany, and a daring plan, the stuff of a contemporary thriller, was devised to get the shipment safely to Ireland and into the hands of the Irish Volunteers. Maybe it is no coincidence that one of those central to the plan, Erskine Childers, had written, just a few years previously, a fast-moving novel called *The Riddle of the Sands*, which involved yachts, spies, and Germans.

This accomplished and misunderstood Englishman, who worked tirelessly for Ireland and eventually gave his life for it, was an experienced yachtsman, and he transported the bulk of the arms in his own rugged yacht, *Asgard*, from a ship off the Belgian coast, around the south coast of England to Howth. His American wife and three companions sailed with him, and together they ran the gauntlet of a British Navy on the alert to expect arms-smuggling, but unlikely to be suspicious of an Englishman on a cruise.

The precision timing of the operation was most impressive. *Asgard* arrived on the high tide at the east pier at Howth at the appointed hour, noon on Sunday, after nineteen days at sea, two of which were spent struggling through a vicious storm that had ripped the mainsail. To ensure that the arms could be distributed immediately on arrival, they had been unpacked and stacked in the cabin, causing considerable discomfort during the passage.

Meeting *Asgard* on the pier of Howth were eight hundred Irish Volunteers and members of Fianna Éireann. They had marched out from Dublin, as they had done on the previous three Sundays to allay any suspicion. Before watching police and coastguards could intervene, the guns were unloaded and the unarmed marchers had become a military force. Once this had happened, the authorities, unaware that none of the ammunition had yet been issued, were unwilling to interfere. Within thirty minutes of *Asgard*'s arrival, the Volunteers had formed up and were marching back to Dublin, and the yacht had sailed out of Howth, bound for Wales. It was to be Erskine Childers's last voyage in his beloved *Asgard*; a week later Germany and Britain were at war and, soon after, as a Reserve officer, he was on active service with the Royal Navy.

Where the east pier joins the mainland near the King Sitric Restaurant, I went into a tiny shop to buy some chocolate, and I spied a guidebook to Howth on a shelf.

'It's a map *and* it's a book,' the shopkeeper told me, using a soft northern sound 'oo' for book. 'It's only recently there, you know. It's a very good read, I believe.'

Outside, I tucked the guide into my knapsack for later reading, and set off uphill along the sea wall. The road overlooks Balscadden Bay, and a steel-grey, angry sea stretched eastwards, breaking explosively against the rugged and rocky coast, a complete contrast to the previous twenty-five miles of sand dunes and mud-flats. Up to the right, on a great promontory of boulder clay, one of the three Martello towers, built to protect the harbour during the Napoleonic Wars, stood out against the sky. I passed by Balscadden House, which, from 1880 to 1883 was the home of the young William Butler Yeats and his family. From here he travelled by train the eight miles to Dublin each day to attend High School. More recently the house was owned by the mother of the rock singer Phil Lynott.

The road veers around towards the east and I ascended an old footpath kerbed and paved with calp, the characteristic black limestone of the Dublin area. A row of tiny cottages was strung along the road, probably originally fishermen's dwellings, but today their location and outlook made them, in spite of their small size, valuable pieces of real estate. For a while some larger Victorian houses perched on the steep hillside below the road blocked the view, until Ireland's Eye came into view again, presenting yet another of its many rugged profiles. Close inshore a rock called the Stag, a great grass-topped monolith, rose out of the sea. Why it is called the stag is hard to say; if it resembles an animal at all, it is a squirrel rather than a stag, bowed down, its head and ears pointing towards the east.

Soon a great thor of burnt volcanic rock loomed ahead, its top two hundred and fifty feet above sea-level. The effect of the summer brush fires that had recently ravaged the Dublin area made the place look as if an eruption had only just subsided. I passed the last few cottages, the satellite dishes and expensive cars parked outside them belying their modesty and, as the road came to an end, I followed a shaly pathway uphill through the bracken. In minutes I had reached the Nose of Howth, the promontory's north-east point, offshore of which a gathering of cormorants were perching on a guano-iced cluster of crags called Puck's Rocks. This part of Howth Head in the autumn is usually a sea of purple heather, the heady perfume of which makes a potent blend with the salt air. But the devastating fires of August had cleared the earth of every blade of grass, herb and shrub, leaving a reddish, dry clay surface, out of which some wizened and blackened furze branches protruded, amidst a scatter of smoke-coated bottles.

Suddenly, as if I had passed through an enchanted door, the north Dublin suburbs and the town of Howth were all left behind, and I found myself in a place apart, walking along high coastal cliffs with a silver sea stretching eastwards to end in a

Paynes Grey meeting with a cloudy sky. In the middle distance was the solitary Kish lighthouse, warning shipping to give a wide berth to the shallowly submerged banks of sand on which it stands. Ahead of me the path led into a wild, new country of rocks and furze. I could just as easily have been walking the cliffs of Minehead in County Waterford, or the rugged shores beyond Dungloe in County Donegal.

The path I was following had been laid down in the nineteenth century by the Great Northern Railway Company as an amenity to be enjoyed by day-trippers to Howth. The granite piers of some of the old stiles, and a few of the original seats, can still be found along the way.

Broad patches of ground inland of the path had also suffered the August fires, revealing ancient long-hidden ditches and banks of earth, some of them with spines of rusted bed-irons that had once carried wire fencing. For some reason the ground near the path was spared in most places, and here the remnants of heather, wild mint, bladderwort, cornflowers, and the dried heads of sea thrift survived amidst bursts of angular, lichen-blotched intrusions of quartzite. But the resilience of nature was evidenced in the midst of the scorched earth, where tiny bright green shoots of brambles and gorse were appearing; even fronds of bracken were asserting themselves, out of season.

As I rounded a promontory, the coast of Wicklow came faintly into view to the south, inland of which the ghostly shapes of the Wicklow Mountains were clustered under an orange sky. Below, every ledge of a reef of foam-margined crags called the Casana Rocks was lined with sea birds, while cormorants swam in their semi-submerged way in the sea swells below, diving repeatedly for fish. It was these rocks that the ill-fated *Queen Victoria*, a passenger steamship out of Liverpool, struck during a thick snowstorm on St Valentine's night 1853. If the vessel had been a sail-only ship, the result of this grounding might not have been so bad. Some of the passengers were able to clamber off the ship on to the rocks before the captain, relying on the relatively new steam-age ability to go astern, reversed the ship off the rocks. As it was pulled back by its great paddle wheels, the original rents in the hull were doubled in size, and the ship rapidly began to fill with water. The boilers became flooded, and without power, the ship drifted south and ran on to the rocks of the Baily promontory, where it sank within fifteen minutes. A passing steamer managed to rescue a good number of the remaining passengers and crew, but about sixty perished. As I stood and looked down on the Casana Rocks, the same sea still beat against the same crags, while offshore an Irish Ferries vessel moved steadily eastwards towards Holyhead, and further south the Stena Sealink Seacat cast up great spumes of white surf as it sped out of Dublin Bay, trailing a long creamy wake.

My old six-inch map named the next cluster of offshore rocks Green Ivy, but there was no ivy to be seen. The meaning of this name, and for other names in the area inscribed on my map, such as Highroom Bed and Gaskins Leap, are probably now lost in the past.

The Baily

One of the most enjoyable things about coast-walking is the frequency of the visual surprises that enliven and shorten the journey, and I rounded another promontory to see, gleaming white, the Baily lighthouse at the tip of a long, low headland stretching to the east. Even from a distance, it was possible to make out the banks and ditches that had been constructed millennia ago to separate the head from the mainland and create a promontory fort called Dun Griffin, the Fort of King Crimthan. He is said to have been King of Ireland at the time of the Roman conquest of Britain, and to have made many plundering attacks on their settlements across the Irish Sea before his death on Howth in A.D. 9.

I passed below the site of the original Howth lighthouse, erected during the reign of Charles II; it consists of a raised beacon fire, and the mound just below the site is made up of cinders. The beacon must have been established by people who were unfamiliar with Howth, because it was sited at such a height on the hill that it was often hidden by fog when conditions at sea-level were clear, and may have caused more shipwrecks than it prevented. The present lighthouse was built in 1814 on the site of Dun Griffin, and during subsequent excavations to extend its accommodation, many human remains were unearthed, probably the casualties of a battle fought on the promontory in A.D. 646.

I followed the path as it descended gently towards the Baily, stopping to pick a few late but very juicy blackberries that were growing in profusion beside the path. A dark-haired, sun-tanned man in his forties who had been coming along behind, also stopped to pick, exclaiming at the sweetness of the berries.

'It's funny', he said, 'that people don't bother picking them any more. They're so good.'

I told him that one of my favourite treats is home-made blackberry and apple tart.

'Down there', he said, 'just across the road, there's an apple tree, so you can actually eat your blackberries, then your apples, and there's a spring where you can have a refreshing drink of lovely cold water as well!'

We laughed at this idea of living off the land, and walked on together. 'You're walking the whole way round I take it?' he asked.

I told him I was.

'The hardest part, the climb, is over you, it just gets a little overgrown further on. We've all been in our shorts here up till last week, so we haven't ventured there lately.'

He was curious about my old six-inch map, and the place names on it. Examining it carefully, he found a house marked which he said had once belonged to his grandfather. I pointed out and admired a palatial house overlooking the Baily, the first dwelling I had seen since leaving Howth Harbour. He said it must be worth a small fortune, because the two terraced lighthouse cottages nearby had recently been sold at auction for two hundred and eighty-five thousand pounds.

We crossed the road leading to the lighthouse and on down a winding pathway that meandered through a leafy-floored tunnel of shrubs. Along the left of the path were gates leading to gardens of houses further up the hill. 'Everyone has a gate on to the path,' my companion said, pointing to one and telling me that it led to Gay Byrne and Kathleen Watkins' garden. I remarked at what a wonderful amenity the cliff walk was for all the people of Howth.

'They and many other residents of Howth today are blow-ins,' he laughed. 'A couple of hundred years ago there were very few people living here, and most of those were descendants of the original Scandinavian settlers. The names are still here. For instance, my grandmother's name was Leland, which is a common name today in Norway.'

We passed a stone on which the polite request, 'Please do not throw stones over cliff', was written in brass letters, and entered a marvellous tunnel through a little copse of *Olearia*, the vigorous daisy bush that does so well near the sea.

'This often becomes completely overgrown,' my companion said. 'We cut back the overgrowth along the right-of-way in winter-time because some of the paths would otherwise become inaccessible. A lot of the properties own the land right down to the shore, or have rights-of-way down to beaches.'

We entered a little wood of conifers, from which there were frequent views to the south, where down the coast, Wicklow Head, the most easterly point of the Republic, was now visible. Further on, from a place my companion said was called Danes Hollow, we could see eastwards to a pair of multifaceted offshore stacks, named on my nineteenth-century map 'The Needles or Candlesticks'. Near these rock outcrops the map indicated what must have been a cave called by the more twentieth-century-sounding name of 'Hippy Hole'.

My acquaintance told me that, as a child, he used to walk this path with his grandfather. One day, when taking a rest on the grass at the side of the path, his grandfather shifted to remove what he thought was a stone under him, and found it to be an old leather purse, full of change. The latest date on the coins was 1900, suggesting that it had waited over fifty years to be found. His grandfather took a detour on the way home and spent the contents of the Victorian lady's purse on a ball of malt for himself and a glass of lemonade for his grandson!

We parted company as my guide turned up a leafy pathway leading inland, shaking hands and wishing me well for the rest of my walk. I followed the path as it turned south towards the Needles and, making my way out on to the cliff-edge above the stacks, eased off my rucksack and sat to have a bite of lunch, already missing my erstwhile companion's chat.

I could see the line of the route I had followed back as far as the Baily, now being picked out by a ray of sunshine, gleaming white against a dark cloud-laden background. Below me a great long open boat puttered along, following the line of the cliffs, its two occupants heaving lobster pots into the sea. Further out, making its way slowly across Dublin Bay, was a strange and ancient-looking vessel, a galleon, complete with stern castle. I had heard that a film was being made about the last High King of Ireland, and reckoned that this vision must have belonged to that operation.

I finished my sandwich and set off again along a path, now bordered with blackthorn, picking a few ripe sloes as I went for dessert. After a short distance the blackthorn gave way to vigorously growing veronica, presumably an escapee from gardens further inland. The path rounded a corner and the pair of high chimneys at the Pigeon House came into view, together with the low-lying and hazy inner shores of Dublin Bay. To the right, a shaft of watery sunshine illuminated the Bull Island, a long pale green and white stripe against the grey sea.

As I came around the west side of Howth and descended towards the shore, there were marked changes in the surrounding rock formations and in the flowers and shrubs. along the way. To my right a long and substantial demesne wall followed the coastline, weaving in and out and falling and rising with the rocky shore. It was a wonderfully constructed wall, using golden Howth stone in a contrasting mortar matrix made with a purple-pink seashore aggregate of broken mussel shells, coloured glass and pebbles. The bottom of the wall was lined with clumps of purple and yellow sea aster and ivory dog roses.

Other than cormorants and gulls, I had not seen many birds on the eastern side of Howth, but now there were plenty about. A flock of oyster-catchers stood on a seaweed-covered hummock of rock protruding from the sea, and a flight of curlews, making that familiar plaintive call, winged over in a vee formation and settled in a field.

I descended to the shore at a place called 'Red Rock' on my map, below a two-hundred-foot-high hillock, where pillows of smooth, shining metamorphosed limestone, glowing pink in the sun, shelved into the sea. Here I found myself a comfortable rock at the water's edge, took off my boots and socks and tested the temperature with my toes. The water was icy cold at first touch, but did not seem as bad as it had been on the west side of Howth when I had last dipped my feet in the sea. I soon acclimatised my blood stream to the temperature and had both feet in the water firmly resting on a pebbly bottom.

It was marvellously peaceful on the shore. The sea had calmed down in the previous few hours, and Dublin Bay was spread out peacefully before me, framed by a horizon that had finally cleared of haze and mist, revealing a familiar mountain skyline to the south. There was no sound in the air but the gentle swish and slosh of tiny waves rustling the stones at the water's edge. I had been pushing it a little for the last couple of miles, anxious to make it as far as Clontarf by the late afternoon. But now, in contact with the rhythm of the sea, I felt myself relaxing, and time began to have little meaning.

Just a few yards offshore a cormorant surfaced, so close I could see the water running off its neck like rivulets of diamonds. It turned its reptilian head, crested with spiked feathers, towards me, and in an instant was gone again, leaving hardly a ripple. I watched for the bird to resurface, and after a couple of minutes it appeared again a hundred yards away.

I gazed into the crystal-clear seawater and daydreamed, wondering at the rich range of colours of the pebbles, rounded and smoothed against each other for centuries by the constant movement of the tides. How often I have taken such jewels home with me in my pocket, only to find that, as in some fairy story, away from the water their lustre and gleam have disappeared, and they have turned again into mere stones.

I eventually had to drag myself away from my dreamy musings at the waterside, and pulling on my socks and boots, continued towards Sutton. The proximity of urban society now was signalled by the plastic bottles, the beer cans and the remains of bonfires in places along the shore. The fires that had ravaged the far side of Howth in August had occurred here too, destroying every stalk of foliage and leaving bare rocks protruding from a scorched, ash-strewn earth. Old iron fence posts, hidden for decades, had also been exposed, undisturbed and exactly as they stood or lay, as if by a painstaking archaeological dig.

Martello tower

The pathway meandered up and down the cliffs, roughly in places, until it finally levelled out and led towards the shore again and a neatly converted Martello tower. Here I reached a gravel road, with a little regret, because it signalled the end of the 'rural' character of my coastal journey. Inland and on higher ground, an elaborate redbrick pile, the Sutton Castle Hotel, rose from a dense woodland. This was originally the home of the Jameson family who owned the whiskey distilleries, which patriotic aficionados of the Irish spirit like to forget were founded in 1770 by a Scotsman. Ahead I saw a silhouette that had first become familiar to me when walking the Waterford coast — a coastguard station watch tower. It terminated in a neat terrace of coastguard cottages, almost identical to similar stations scattered along all the coasts of Ireland. As I came up to it I saw that it had been lovingly restored,

with the roof retiled and the walls painted white. I stopped to take
a photograph of it, just as a dapper, elderly man came down the
garden path.

'It's an old coastguard cottage,' he said.

I told him I had recognised it as one, having seen many around
the country.

'So have I, but d'you know there are no two the same, it's
something that always puzzles me. I mean you would have
thought they would have been built to some Board of Works plan,
but I've never seen two the same. The grandest of all I suppose is
the one at Dun Laoghaire. There is a wonderful museum of the
coastguard some place on the south coast of England which I must
visit. It's on my list, but I haven't got to it yet. The coastguards left
here about 1909; an elderly man called one day years ago and told
me he had been stationed here as a young man. D'you know, I was
in a hurry that day, and only had time to show him around and
talk to him briefly. I have regretted ever since not taking more
time with him; the things he could have told me!'

I chatted with him a little longer and he pointed out a good
photograph would be one that includes all the chimneys of the
terrace. I clambered on to a wall and got the picture he
recommended, before I said goodbye and continued on my way.
Behind the cottages stood a fine late-Georgian house, called on
the old map Sea Lawn; it looks as if the lawns in front of it might
have originally swept down to the sea. As I carried on, more
recently built houses increased in number at the roadside,
interspersed with well-maintained Victorian and Georgian villas.
There was no sign of a dolomite mine that was worked here in
the middle of the nineteenth century, from where magnesitic
limestone was exported to England.

The eastern shore of the Bull Island was not far away now,
across the mud-flats left by the receding tide, through which the
waters of Sutton Creek meandered. At the margins of the creek,

flocks of geese and waders fed vigorously before the tide would come in again to replenish the larder. In strong westerly winds the shore becomes eroded here, and someone had been dumping stone and concrete along the water's edge as a storm wall. In the midst of a confusion of concrete slabs, I came across portions of an ornately carved pediment of classical style in Portland stone. I hunted around and soon found more pieces, some of which were clearly parts of a great door architrave, complete with delicate acanthus leaves and scrolls. I could not understand how such beautiful pieces of work could end up dumped here, surrounded with base concrete; but for their great weight, I would have taken them home to the garden and built myself a little folly!

At Sutton Cross I reached tarmac again, where a yellow, hand-lettered sign hanging on a lamp post informed me that there was a jumble sale in the parish hall nearby starting at two o'clock. I had taken quite a long rest at Red Rock, so rather than increase my pace in order to get to Clontarf by late afternoon, I decided to pay a visit to the sale. I followed the road as it turned away from the shore and reached the hall, bedecked with flags and bunting, after a few minutes.

A large sign promised bric-à-brac, cakes, good-as-new-clothes, books and something called tombola. The doors were not yet open and I joined a queue of about a dozen people waiting outside. In front of me were a tiny elderly couple, a little gent and his wife, both carrying equally old oilcloth shopping bags. His dapper navy suit and tweed cap were only partly taken from by the white runners on his feet; he wore a fresh pink rosebud in his lapel. She was wearing an oversized coat of a shade of turquoise that must have made it almost unmarketable when it was in the shop, with an imitation leopard-skin collar. On her head she had an imitation mink turban. Where do they rear all these imitation animals? I mused silently.

In front of the couple, a covey of track-suited women with

curlers in their hair were chatting, while innumerable young children and near infants chased noisily in and out between them. I overheard mention of further Sales of Work that day, which were the best for clothes, and which were good for tins of food.

A middle-aged, well-dressed blonde woman with large rings on both hands joined the queue behind me with a much younger clone of herself who must have been her daughter. They were carrying large, capacious shopping bags.

The woman at the head of the queue was becoming agitated; she could see into the hall by standing on the tips of her toes, and was excited by what she saw. 'It's gone two o'clock,' she announced to everyone, pointing to her Swatch watch. She was a round-faced woman with hair dyed such a strange light brown colour that it looked as if she had borrowed it. Her brow was wrinkling with impatience as she said, 'It's well gone two o'clock,' pointing to her watch again and giving the varnished Victorian door a slap. Everyone smiled and, out of solidarity, a good-natured chant began of, 'Open up, open up, open up!'

The door opened a crack and a grey face peered out, as the queue surged forward, the mother and daughter team seeming to go through me; one minute they were behind me, the next in front.

'The stalls are not ready,' the face in the crack called, and promptly closed the door. General murmuring began as the woman at the front whipped up an indignation in the queue: 'It's nearly half two already. What are they doing?' She slapped on the door again.

Suddenly the door was open all the way, and I was left behind as the queue moved forward in a body and promptly became wedged in the doorway. After some moments the log-jam was freed, and I began to move with the flow. Inside the porch of the hall a gangly seventy-year-old, the face in the crack, belied his age by the strength with which he corralled the punters into a single line leading to another man sitting at a table on which was a tin box. He was taking the entrance fee, all of thirty pence. I pitied the agitated lady in front of me because he was taking an eternity to count out, in small coinage, the exact change due from the pound she had proffered.

By the time I got into the hall, all hell had broken loose; around each stall devotees were feverishly rummaging amongst its offerings, watched over by sternly proprietorial stall-holders. I made my way to the book stall, where a disparate gathering was perusing rows of volumes laid out on a table.

I ignored the frenzied activity going on all round, by-passed the paperbacks and browsed through the hardbacks which were gathered together at the end of the stall. A rich array of titles and subjects faced me: obscure technical manuals, probably dangerously out-of-date, Victorian novels with gloriously decorated boards, religious tracts, colourful biographies of Royalty, old gardening books with hand-coloured photographs, and lots of travel literature. Although there were many intriguing works I would have happily bought, I limited myself to three: *The Book of Inishowen*, *The History of European Fauna* and *The Saturday Book for 1952*, and held them aloft for one of the stall-holders to assess. I had noticed that the three men tending the book stall seemed to use different methods for arriving at a price. One looked carefully and at length at all the titles, as if they would give a clue to the value of the book. Another seemed to count the books a few times before coming up with a figure. My vendor carefully flicked through the pages of each book as if to make a final check that there was not a tenner hiding between the pages, and then apologetically asked for one pound and fifty pence, a pittance, which I quickly paid in case he might change his mind.

A man next to me was examining books with a magnifying glass. At first I thought he was examining the details of the bindings, but then I realised he was very short-sighted. 'That's a nice one you got there,' he said in a strong Dublin accent, without looking at me. He was dressed in an old gabardine coat with a long tweed scarf wound around his neck a few times. I asked which one he meant, and he turned to me, pointed at my bundle, and said '*The Book of Inishowen*, it has some nice photos from the 1930s. I was looking at it a few minutes ago.'

He dropped his voice, 'D'you know they're charging two pounds each for the dog-eared paperbacks up the other end!' He laughed. 'I was at the Silesian Fathers last week and when I asked why there were no hardbacks, the wan on the stall told me she had thrown them all out the back, because they never sell. I rushed out and rescued a big box of them from the rain, and she gave me it for a pound!'

At the other end of the stall, under the eye of the slightly disapproving but helpless stall-holders, a man was flinging all the glossy and fat paperbacks he could find into a cardboard box without so much as looking at the titles.

'He's a dealer,' my neighbour told me. 'He'll be sellin' those books at a huge profit next week.'

His head ducked again and he continued his minute examination of the contents of the stall. I wandered off, passing the little gent I had seen in the queue, standing in the middle of the room feeling foolish with a huge lampshade in one hand, a trouser press under the other arm, and the oilcloth bag stuffed with rhubarb and women's magazines between his feet. The tombola advertised on the posters turned out to be a kind of ticket raffle, with the winning numbers being selected by a great rattling multicoloured wheel. The stage behind the wheel was covered with glossy and garish prizes of all sorts, from teddy bears to six-packs of Coke. As I watched, the spinning wheel slowed to a stop, and there was a flurry in the knot of gamblers clutching tickets gathered in front of it, until one curlered woman screeched something and ran up to the man on the stage. She selected a pink fur-lined wastepaper basket as her prize and, putting it proudly with a bundle of other purchases on the lap of a child in a push-chair, went off through the crowd, followed by two other children.

Leaving the hall and the excited hubbub, I stepped out into the road again and made my way towards Sutton Cross and a bus into Dublin.

6

Sutton to the Liffey

Early the following morning I was dropped at Sutton Cross to take up where I had left off. It was nearly December and the winter was hunting out a late autumn with cold rains and freezing winds. I was anxious to complete my journey as far as the Liffey before taking a break for the cold season, and hoped, to cover the distance from Sutton into town that day, even though there was much of interest en route to dally over.

I walked east to reach the recently constructed pedestrian and cycle track that runs between the coast road and the sea, all the way into Fairview. The coast road to Dublin from Howth was originally surveyed by Thomas Telford, the prolific engineer dubbed by the poet Southey 'The Colossus of Roads', in the early nineteenth century. It was constructed as part of the same contract as the great Holyhead and London road, to carry the mails from the new packet station at Howth, and was sometimes spoken of as the 'Dublin and London road'. Telford had prepared designs for roads and harbours up the east coast of Ireland from Waterford to Donaghadee a few years before, and had applied, without success, to become engineer to the Board of Control of the Irish Inland Waterways. He seems not to have enjoyed his Irish sojourn: in 1817 he commented in a letter, 'I . . . spent six weeks in the Metropolis of Pat's Country; I must confess it enables me to set a higher Value on our own.'

I made my way along the pedestrian path, weaving to avoid the minefield of dog droppings littering it. The open sea was lost to sight behind low and green Bull Island, separated from the mainland by a calm lagoon. Inland, across the road, was a seeming endless parade of bungalows, most of them built since World War II.

I was relieved to reach the ruins of Kilbarrack Church, which interrupted the sequence, although it took quite a few minutes to get a safe gap in the speeding traffic to cross the road to this oasis. Not much remains of the old church, which was once called the Chapel of Mone, indicating ancient connections with the Isle of Anglesey, for which it is an old name. The washed-up dead of many shipwrecks lie in the burial ground, most in unmarked graves; the earliest tombstone I found carried a date of 1755. A fine modern stone particularly drew my attention, erected to a Bernie Brennan, who, from the wonderfully carved figure on the back of the stone of an angler in the process of casting, must have been a very keen fisherman. A flock of tumbling pigeons circled the graveyard in graceful flight, launching every few circuits into a series of joyful aerobatics.

I crossed the road again and continued beside the shore towards the causeway that links the eastern end of Bull Island with the mainland. Its construction in the 1970s brought a storm of protest from wildlife associations, which claimed that it would lead to the destruction of the salt mud-flats between the island and the mainland, and would ruin what is, because of its proximity to the city centre, an internationally unique urban wild-bird reserve. Apparently what was feared did not happen, and the area continues to attract a wondrous bird population. There is no other capital city I know of where you can stand on the roadside and see such species as goldeneye duck, red-breasted mergansers, widgeon, teal pintails and a host of others; counts of ten thousand knot, nine thousand dunlin and five thousand oyster-catchers have been made here.

I passed an ugly graffiti-covered building surrounded by litter, a blot on the landscape. A sign proclaimed that it was the Kilbarrack Scouts Den, a poor advertisement for that organisation. Further on, the reservation between the road and the sea broadened to a grassy border, and a screen of palm trees helped to cut down the noise of the traffic. When I reached the causeway to Bull Island, I stopped to consider my options: I could either cross to the island and walk down Dollymount Strand, returning to the mainland at Clontarf, or continue along the shore, taking in the heavily treed demesne of St Anne's Park, which I could see ahead. I decided on the park, crossed the road again and passed through a gateway on to a pathway lined with holm oaks.

I cannot think of any place where I have seen as many holm oaks. The tree was introduced from the Mediterranean into the British Isles in the sixteenth century, and it became popular as a parkland tree in the early Victorian period. When young, its prickly evergreen leaves resemble those of the holly, which probably accounts for its Latin name, *quercus ilex*, which means holly oak. Another species growing in abundance in the park was the traditional yew. We have become accustomed to the vertical Irish variety that one sees in churchyards, all of which are descendants of a single seedling grown in County Fermanagh in the eighteenth century, but the original species has a more normal tree shape. The innumerable yews and holm oaks lining the paths frequently created dark tunnels blocking out all sunlight.

St Anne's Park is what remains of a fine demesne and gardens laid out in the 1830s and '40s by Benjamin Lee Guinness, around a palatial eleven-bay house. On his death, St Anne's passed to his eldest son, Arthur, as did Ashford Castle in County Galway. Arthur had little interest in the brewing business, and was subsequently bought out by his younger brother, Edward, for six hundred and eighty thousand pounds, a king's ransom in 1876. Edward, who was soon to become Lord Iveagh, had a good business head, and four years later sold the brewery into public ownership for six million pounds.

Arthur was responsible for the opening of St Stephen's Green to the public in 1880, having spent twenty thousand pounds of his own money on the remodelling works, much of which he designed himself. Landscaping was one of his passions, something he shared with his wife Olive, and the vast estate at Ashford, and to a lesser extent the gardens of St Anne's, gave plenty of scope for the exercise of their talents. At St Anne's the gardens included lakes, a tea-house modelled on a Pompeiian temple, a replica of a house from the recently excavated Roman town of Herculaneum, and a walled garden setting for statues brought back from Italy.

The house was considerably extended in the 1870s and '80s to include a new entrance wing, a double-height ballroom with a gallery, and a roof-lit palm court rising to the full height of the building.

Arthur was eventually knighted for his services, and subsequently raised to the peerage as Lord Ardilaun, while St Anne's became legendary for its garden parties and balls. After Lord Ardilaun's death in 1902, Lady Ardilaun continued the garden parties, but the great house was cold and draughty, and she took to spending the winter months in her house on St Stephen's Green. By the time she died in 1925, the house had not been lived in for some time, and since Lord and Lady Ardilaun had no children, the property was inherited by the Right Reverend John Plunkett, the Bishop of Meath. He had little use for such a palatial house, and put the property and four-hundred-and-eighty-four-acre estate up for sale in 1932. A buyer could not be found, however, over the ensuing seven years, and eventually, in 1939, Dublin Corporation bought the house and estate for fifty-five thousand pounds.

An auction of the considerable contents of the house was arranged for October 1939, but the declaration of war on 3

September intervened, and in the midst of collapsing prices, the sale was brought forward three weeks. It was too late, however, and during the sale many rare works of art were sold for a song.

I came across a catalogue of that auction in an unusual place. I was cruising on the Barrow with a friend during the month of August a few years ago. We moored the boat at Milltown Bridge one evening, and walked up to the town of Borris for a drink. On the outskirts of the town there seemed to be a lot of traffic, and we saw a strange notice posted on the lawn in front of a house, proclaiming, 'Grass poisoned: unsuitable for grazing'! Further on were more signs with similar messages; one stated that the garden wall was also poisoned. Along the road strange objects such as pieces of wrought iron, a broken chair and an old dog's kennel had been placed near the pavement.

Within minutes the reason for these strange phenomena became clear. We passed a number of itinerants' caravans parked beside the road and people setting up stalls beside them to sell clothes, lengths of wire, and a myriad other articles, all second-hand, and some very much the worse for wear. Further on we saw that even the forecourt to the imposing neo-gothic gateway of Borris House was crammed with caravans and stalls, and on down the long main street, many more, on both sides of the road. And all around, itinerants young and old were bustling about carrying prams, armfuls of old clothes, horse brasses, and cardboard boxes of artefacts difficult to identify or describe. Each family was setting up its selling patch.

The annual Fairday had come to Borris, we were told by one of four Guards patrolling the street. Annually, on 15 August, every traveller in the south-east of Ireland descends on Borris to meet their relations and friends and sell all the junk that they have collected over the previous twelve months. It had traditionally been a general livestock fair, where travellers, farmers and livestock dealers would gather from the surrounding countryside to buy and sell animals and goods. Changing farming practices, and the influence of the European Union, however, had long ago seen an end of such sociable events, and the travellers found that they had only themselves to compete with for space on the main street. The competition for a stand as near the centre of the village as possible was very keen. Those who had not assembled or loaded their merchandise in time sent emissaries ahead to the town to claim a good location on the street by placing some object on the road a couple of feet from the footpath; this was the reason for the collection of obstructions we had seen earlier. This practice invariably led to arguments as to who had left what, and what length of street was being claimed, and the disagreement was often resolved by a fight, which explained the Guards' presence.

Everything imaginable was for sale. Not a thing I saw was new and most items had satisfied many more than one owner before reaching the street of Borris. Boxes of old, well-thumbed paperbacks were piled high on mountains of multi-coloured broken plastic toys. Ornately framed and garishly coloured holy pictures lay beside images of green oriental women and white horses galloping through the surf of a blue sea. Fascinating collections of out-of-date tools, for doing just about every job, shared footpath space with piles of assorted nails and screws, grommets and washers, used light bulbs and old wellington boots.

Among a number of dog-eared Harold Robbins paperbacks, I came across a large hardbacked book with a crest and the title 'St Anne's, Clontarf, Dublin' engraved on the cover. Before I really knew what it was, I asked the rosy-cheeked girl at the stall how much she wanted for the book. 'A pound,' she said immediately, and when I suggested fifty pence, she just as fast agreed and took the coin.

It turned out to be the catalogue of the 1939 sale of the contents of St Anne's and was a gem of a find, particularly since whoever had owned it had pencilled in many of the prices that the items fetched. There were nearly two thousand lots in the sale, which lasted for ten days, and the prices paid seem ludicrously low. One of the highest prices, two hundred pounds, was paid for an old Waterford glass chandelier, which today hangs in the National Gallery, while a life-size marble sculpture of a reclining figure executed in 1846 by the Waterford sculptor John Hogan was sold for twenty-eight pounds; it now graces Iveagh House. A Rubens painting went for twenty-five pounds, and a Millais and a Van Dyck went for forty pounds and twenty pounds respectively!

The catalogue had stimulated my interest in the house and demesne, which was one of the reasons I had chosen to take this route to Clontarf rather than along Dollymount Strand. I knew that the house had been demolished in the late 1960s, but wondered what, if anything, remained of it.

A few minutes after entering the park, I noticed, scattered at the foot of the trees lining the pathway and partially colonised by ivy, many blocks of stone. They seemed to be sandstone and limestone remnants of elaborately carved ornate door and window linings, including the curved stones of one or more arches, and the unmistakable mullions of a gothic window. I counted up to fifty of these cut-stone pieces along a stretch of path thirty metres long.

I walked on, curious to see if I could identify the site of the house, from which I guessed these sad remains had come. A network of leafy paths wended their way between hillocks of earth on which little grew because of the shade of the oaks and yews, and I followed one until it brought me over a stone foot-bridge spanning a tiny trickling stream and out into a broad and beautiful tree-bordered parkland.

The parkland was bisected by a long and straight tree-lined avenue more than a mile long. At the end nearest to me was a flat-topped grassy mound which I guessed was all that remained of St Anne's House; the volume of the mound suggested that it had been a very big building indeed. Nearby, half-hidden in the trees at the edge of the open space, I spotted some ruins. A classical doorway flanked by two arched niches led into what must have been a tiny tea-house, which terminated in a semi-circular veranda, the coffered roof supported by six Portland stone Ionic columns. The building was perched on an artificial cliff made from great strata-like blocks of limestone overhanging a slow-moving stream, and the remains of a stone arch suggested that the veranda once led on to a footbridge. The columns and cut-stone wall linings were heavily decorated with graffiti, but gentle graffiti, indicating romantic attachments, rather than the obscenities more commonly seen.

Folly in St Anne's Park

I clambered down into the stream bed to get a photograph of the folly, but I slipped on the muddy slope. My feet went from under me and slid straight into the shallow water as I sat down with a thump. Luckily, the braking effect of my bottom hitting the ground stopped the progress of my feet before the water had reached the top of my boots. I clambered back again with nothing hurt but my pride.

I followed another path through a carved limestone opening in an ivy-clad wall and found myself in what had been, fifty years before, an ornate formal garden designed around a pond. What must have once been a circular yew hedge was now a ring of scraggy yew trees surrounding the stone lined pond, which had become a circular copse of elder bushes. Nearby an enormous cedar, seemingly unaffected by attempts to kill it by mutilation and fire, stretched skyward a tangle of huge branches.

Nearby I found another grotto of great boulders forming an arch, beyond which were a set of formal granite steps leading me back to the open parkland and the grassy mound. From this angle I could see the top of a clock tower between the trees further down the great avenue, and I went to investigate. The tower stood over an arched brick gateway with a padlocked gate, beyond which lay a beautiful, pristine formal walled garden. Nearby sat an elderly white-moustached man, sprucely dressed in a navy suit with waistcoat under a tweed coat. I asked him when the walled garden was open to the public.

He told me that they opened it only for an hour or two in the mornings. I asked him about the big house, and if my guess about the mound was correct.

'The big mansion? Yes, it's the hump in the ground at the end of the avenue. It was a huge mansion. There were underground tunnels down to the lake there. You could walk to the kitchens under the ground.'

I asked him if he remembered the people who lived there.

'Of course I do.' He emphasised his words by tapping his walking stick on the ground. 'I remember Lord Ardilaun and Lady Ardilaun when they were here. It was a wonderful place; the walls must have been four feet thick. Actually Guinnesses owned it. Lord Ardilaun was one of the Guinnesses, and then Bishop Plunkett came. It was used as a store during the war; they kept gas-masks and boots and dungarees and uniforms there. Some said that they stored whiskey as well. I knew the man that was the caretaker; he lived in the grounds here, and he was fond of the gargle but he never said anything about there being whiskey stored. They say that for years there was some hookery going on: they was floggin' boots and shirts and things; there were fellas who weren't in the army walkin' the streets dressed in army gear. I mean, money was hard to come by; there was no money around then. But when the war finished, the whole thing was going to be scaled down. There was going to be a big check-up, and when my friend was down in the pub on a Saturday night — well, he couldn't be on duty twenty-four hours a day — a fire started in the kitchens, and the place was burnt down.'

He was silent for a few moments, gazing into space, and then he looked up at me and said, 'People didn't know; they didn't realise the value of these things then, and the place was bulldozed. I mean, where that mansion was now, there was a walk there put in by Lady Ardilaun, all the way down to Mount Prospect Avenue. It had big high hedges on either side, and there would be tombstones for her dogs along it, with their names cut on them, like "Freda, my favourite Irish Wolfhound". Over the years as her dogs died, she always put up a stone to them, and some of them were big. It was a lovely walk on the high ground, you could look out over the sea. Everyone used to walk along it after the place was taken over. The hedges were pulled out of it in a day with a bulldozer. It wasn't realised then; it was only years afterwards that people learned about the value of these things.'

He stretched himself and said, as if he was tired of talking now, and wanted me to be on my way, 'You should go and see the rose-garden put in by the Corporation. There's not much growing now, but it's worth a look.'

I thanked him and went across the avenue to a formally laid out garden of rosebeds and pergolas. Although few of the roses were in bloom, their names, noted on metal plates in front of each bed, made fascinating reading. Jeanne de Montfort was opposite York and Lancaster, Centifolia Christata and Robert le Diable grew very close together, and Buff Beauty seemed to enjoy the company of Frau Dagmar Hasstrupp. The garden was a long oval shape on two levels, with seats arranged about regularly on neat cobble platforms; the perfumes on a calm summer evening must be wonderful.

A large, bald, elderly man and a younger woman were sitting on one of the seats. I asked them how long the rose garden had been established. They told me it had been built sometime in the 1970s, and when I mentioned the old house, the man said emphatically, 'That was a disgrace, that was a disgrace! I was in that house, I was, and as a young lad I got many a chase out of the place, I'll tell you that!'

He laughed. 'There were lovely fireplaces in the house, and big greenhouses out the back, about fifty feet high.'

He repeated what my previous informant had told me about the original ownership, but he had a wonderful-sounding way of saying 'Lord Ardilaun' in true Dublinese. It is difficult to reproduce on paper, but he pronounced it as Lord Ardle-awn, the 'dle' pronounced by touching the tongue against the front of the roof of the mouth and expelling air out both sides.

'Bishop Plunkett moved to St Paul's College up here. That was his house when he sold this. St Anne's was a beautiful house, second to none, the night it went on fire. The time of the day it went on fire was interesting; the tide was out, you see, so there was no water to put out the fire. There was little bits and buts about why it happened at all and what started it. It's a mystery, it was always a mystery, it's a mystery still.'

'I only remember it when it was a burnt-out wreck,' the woman said. 'They were thinking of rebuilding it one time as a restaurant or something, but there is nothing there now apart from the mound. They could have made something out of it; it's such a pity.'

'But it's great all the same', the man said, 'that the park belongs to the people now, and the Corporation got it for a song. The Guinnesses were always very good like that; they gave Stephen's Green and that as well at a price, practically little or nothing, you know. That's why I keep drinking their pints!' He roared with laughter.

I left them laughing and headed back towards the coast road along the west side of the park. On the way I came to a large and beautiful redbrick, Tudor-style building with a gothic pinnacle in carved limestone, that seemed to be the Corporation's administrative centre of the park. They were originally the stables of St Anne's, and their elaborate design and the craftsmanship with which they are built leaves one wondering at how magnificent the original mansion was. In the stable yard a man was tutoring six other men in the fine art of chain sawing. They all looked strangely alien in their fluorescent yellow waterproofs and large shining earmuffs, like Mickey Mouse ears. A grass-cutting machine as large as a combine harvester, and another just as big — for what purpose I could not guess, occupied the yard which a hundred years ago would have resounded with the clop of horses' hoofs and the rattle of carriage wheels on cobbles.

Just before leaving the park, I passed another folly that resembled a Norman tower house. A plaque on it tells much of the story of the ownership of St Anne's:

THIS TOWER AND BRIDGE WAS ERECTED IN 1838
BY SIR BENJAMIN LEE GUINNESS BART MP
TO COMMEMORATE THE BIRTH OF HIS ELDEST CHILD
ANNIE LEE BORN AT ST ANNE'S CLONTARF, JUNE 11TH 1838,
MARRIED JUNE 11TH 1863 WILLIAM CONYGHAM PLUNKETT
FOURTH BARON PLUNKETT, LORD ARCHBISHOP OF DUBLIN
LORD PLUNKETT DIED AT OLD CONNAUGHT HOUSE BRAY
NOVEMBER 8TH 1889

THIS INSCRIPTION WAS PLACED HERE
BY SIR BENJAMIN GUINNESS,
GRANDSON AND LADY PLUNKETT'S SON RIGHT REVEREND
THE HONORABLE BENJAMIN JOHN PLUNKETT DD BISHOP, 1926

Passing out on to the road beside a wonderfully flamboyant gate lodge, I left behind a park of mysteries, intrigue, elegant ruins and leafy walks. My later researches revealed that the house had indeed been an ARP (Air Raid Precautions) store during the 'Emergency', and in 1943 it was partially destroyed by fire. What remained was vandalised over the years, and, like many other local authorities when faced with a similar problem, Dublin Corporation lacked the imagination and the money to do anything other than demolish the building. This was done in 1968. It was one of many houses around the perimeter of Dublin to suffer similar fates during the explosion of suburbia in the 1960s and '70s, before a new era dawned, and, as the first man had said, 'people learned about the value of these things'.

I was back in the noisy world of speeding vehicles again, an extreme contrast from the leafy glades of St Anne's. This section of road, called James Larkin Road, once a laneway, must have been one of the first modern road developments in the Dublin area when it was built in 1949. Straight ahead, beyond the roof-tops and spires of Dublin, the sky to the west of the mountains looked ominous, and I wondered if I would reach Clontarf before it rained. I was getting a little footsore after my wanderings in the park; I had spent almost two hours there and was feeling peckish. I decided to find a suitable pub where I could get something to eat.

By the age of some of the houses I was passing, a number of which seemed to be early nineteenth century, it was clear that I had now reached the outskirts of an older Dublin. Others, indicated and named on my map, had disappeared, such as Lakeview Cottage, presumably so named because it overlooked Crablake Water, the now disused name for the stretch of water between the shore and Bull Island.

After passing a series of Edwardian sea-front terraces, I came, with some relief, to a pub called Dollymount House, a place where the warmth, the smell of tobacco smoke and beer, the clink of glasses and the hum of conversation immediately had a restful effect. It was large, with a decor of mirrors, dark wood, stained glass panels and triffid-like artificial plants hanging from the ceiling. I queued at the food counter and got myself a plate of roast beef, potatoes and carrots, and a glass of Guinness.

The food was most welcome, and the stout delicious. The place, in spite of its size, had a friendly and homely atmosphere, with groups of chatting people seated in alcoves, and walls and pillars hung with such seafaring memorabilia as brass portholes and posters advertising sales of the contents of wrecked ships. It would have been easy to stay in the comfortable seat and watch the comings and goings, but I still had some way to go before evening closed in, so I slung my rucksack on my back and left the cosy pub.

The timber-floored bridge out to Bull Island was the next landmark. It is difficult to accept that this substantial island, an amenity for countless thousands of Dubliners, did not exist two hundred years ago. It came into being following attempts to improve the access for shipping into the Liffey. Two centuries ago, the Liffey and the Dodder flowed into Dublin Bay by way of a channel through extensive sandbanks which were generated by the actions of the tides up and down the Irish Sea. The constant roaring of the tidal waters on these banks led to them being named the North Bull and the South Bull. (Clontarf, the Meadow of the Bull, is said to refer to one of these bulls.) The channel, however, was constantly changing in position and depth, creating a great hazard for shipping, so during the eighteenth century the Great South Wall was constructed to shelter the channel from the south. It was, in its size and its engineering achievement, one of the most remarkable constructions in the western world at the time, and in view of the state of ignorance of the science of hydrology, an enormous gamble on the behalf of the radical

Ballast Board, which had responsibility, as the Harbour Board does now, for the port's development. The great wall is still extant, although much of it has been swallowed by land reclaimed from the sea, but at the time it was built it extended out from Ringsend into the bay for a distance of three and a half miles.

Although the Great South Wall improved matters considerably, there remained some difficulties on the north side of the bay. Various engineers and naval officers, including Captain Bligh, ex-master of *The Bounty*, who was attached to Dublin Harbour for a time, were consulted for solutions to the problem. One of the proposals was the construction of another wall about a mile long, starting at Clontarf, and this work was carried out and completed in 1824. It withstood the depredations of the sea and resulted in a much improved navigable channel into the Liffey, and fortuitously, the emergence of Bull Island.

As new land emerged from the bay, marram grasses took hold, stabilising the sands, followed by grasses, herbs and hardy shrubs. The seaward side became a broad beach, an amenity that attracted first the residents of the area, and subsequently, when a horse-drawn tram service from the city to Dollymount began in 1873, it became a Dublin watering place. Lines of colourful, privately owned bathing machines appeared along the beach; bathers who had not the wherewithal to enjoy such facilities undressed in the open and drew complaints to the Harbour Board of 'the primitive, not to say indecent, exhibitions taking place there'. The increased use of the timber bridge connecting the Bull Wall and thereby Bull Island to the mainland, originally built to enable the wall to be constructed, led to deterioration, and the Harbour Board at one stage proposed the bridge's removal, but reconsidered the matter because of the consequent public outcry.

Such was the extent and maturity of the grasslands on the island that by the early 1920s two golf clubs had been established, the Royal Dublin and St Anne's. In 1931 the island was designated a bird sanctuary, and with the variety of habitats it offers, it is today a mecca for bird-watchers; the mud-flats alone provide feeding for six thousand wildfowl and twenty-five thousand waders.

When I was at school, the most important date in Irish history was 1014, the year of the battle of Clontarf. In those simple days we believed it to have been a contest between all that is good and all that is evil; the Christian Irish led by their brave king, Brian Boru, against the foreign and pagan Danes. Of course the reality was not so simple, and if there had been newspapers in those days, they would have had a field day with the power-plays, intrigues, sexual jealousy and murders that led up to the battle.

The Scandinavians, formerly the feared sea-pirates who sacked many an Irish settlement and monastery, had by the eleventh century established trading settlements throughout the British Isles. Most of the coastal cities of Ireland were founded by the Northmen, and from these bases, through their trading, they exerted a strong and growing influence on the country. At the time, Ireland was made up of a disunited and unprogressive series of small kingdoms which would have been unable to withstand the subtle influence of the foreigners had it not been for two exceptional rulers who came to power at the time. Maelaughlin became High King in 980 and carried on a successful opposition to the political ambitions of the Scandinavians. In 998 he joined with the Munster king, Dalcaissean Brian Boru, to deal a series of defeats on the foreigners, before he himself was deposed by Brian.

By 1014, the power of the Scandinavians had re-established itself, and Brian Boru, now in his seventies, moved to break their influence in Ireland for good. The High King marched his armies from the south on the Danish city of Dublin, burning all the way, as was the custom of the time, so that the lights of the fires filled the night sky. Battle was joined on Good Friday at Clontarf where a main force of Scandinavians, a fleet of ships from the Orkneys and the Isle of Man, came ashore. The slaughter that took place

114

inspired many sagas and songs in both traditions, and the details of the battle are blurred by the legends. It seems, however, that the fighting took place in a series of bloody skirmishes along the forest-fringed shore of Dublin Bay from the mouth of the Tolka to Castle Avenue; many of the invaders were drowned when they were driven back into the rising tide. By the end of the day the casualties included Jarl Sigurd, King of Orkney, and Brian Boru, but the Scandinavians had been routed.

The battle is remembered in place-names like Danesfort Road and Brian Boru Avenue, but while Brian Boru's Well is preserved in Castle Avenue, I was disappointed to find that many other places and names reminiscent of the battle, such as Conquer Hill and Conquer Terrace, have disappeared within the last fifty years.

As the coast began to swing around to the right, the centre of old Clontarf village came into view, and I crossed the road to see how it had fared over the last eighty years since my map had been printed. Fort View Villa, a four-bayed late Georgian or early Victorian dwelling, still existed, now named Fort View House. The Fort in the name was the Pigeon House Fort on the South Wall opposite, clearly visible when the house was built, but now obscured by the twentieth-century port. A Planning Permission notice nailed to a sycamore tree in the front garden indicated that plans were afoot to demolish the place and build ten apartments.

Beyond this were a series of elegant Victorian terraces, with good Victorian names like Alexandra Terrace and Rutland Terrace, some with fine bow-fronted windows, others looking in need of refurbishment. These terraces led me to Vernon Avenue, where the old Clontarf fishing village was once located. Inland from here was a district which was known by the quaint name of the 'Green Lanes'. Up to fifty years ago the junction between Vernon Avenue and Clontarf Road was called Clontarf Sheds, after the herring curing sheds that lined the shore here; the name was probably not up-market enough to be taken on by the pharmacy, building society, and Chinese restaurant now occupying the place. A little further along a rich oyster-bed called the Furlong used to extend southwards from the shore.

I crossed back to the seaward side of the road and passed the Clontarf Baths, a dilapidated collection of dirty white walls and steps extending out into the water. The treed demesnes, shown on my old maps to have existed on either side of Castle Avenue, are today densely filled with apartment blocks. Their view across the river to the south and the mountains must be marred by the ugly collection of chimneys, oil storage tanks, and industrial buildings that fill the foreground on a recently created promontory of land dividing the outlet of the Liffey from that of the Tolka river.

It is difficult to visualise what Dublin Bay looked like a couple of centuries ago before the hundreds of acres of new land occupied by the industrial port were reclaimed from the bay. Offshore here, splitting the outflow of the Tolka, there was once a narrow strip of land called Clontarf Island, about a third of a mile long. It became a summer resort and took on the name of Bathing Island in the nineteenth century when bathing became popular, and a regular Bathing Island Ferry barge plied out to it from Clontarf. There was at least one summer-house on the island until the night of 9 October 1844, when the most powerful storm recorded in Dublin's annals washed it away. Subsequent to the erection of the Great Northern Railway embankment across the inner bay in 1843 and the resultant changes to the complex hydraulics influencing the bay, the island was steadily eroded, and by the end of the nineteenth century it had been reduced to a faint, stony-surfaced sandbank.

Far in the distance the new East Stand at Croke Park, towering over the north side of the city, made an impressive new Dublin landmark, joining a skyline that featured the spire of St George's Church, Liberty Hall and the Wellington monument in the Phoenix Park.

If I were keeping to a rule of staying by the shore, I would have turned south at Alfie Byrne Road to head across the East Wall, but the rules were mine to make up as I went along, so I kept on straight under the railway bridge into Fairview. The red sandstone pinnacles of Fairview church glowed warmly and wonderfully in a wayward sunbeam as I passed by and crossed the Malahide road. To my right, hidden from the main road by trees, is Marino Crescent, which, when completed in the late 1790s, was close to the seashore. When the building of the houses commenced, the owner of Marino House further inland, Lord Charlemont, was concerned that they would interfere with his sea-view, and he tried to prevent their completion by charging exorbitant tolls on the materials, which had to be transported through his land. The builder, however, had his materials brought across Dublin Bay by barge, and delivered on to the shore, and completed the terrace so that the view from Marino House was completely blocked.

William Carleton, the novelist and essayist, lived in No. 2, Marino Crescent in the 1840s, and Bram Stoker, author of *Dracula*, was born in No. 15 in 1847.

As I walked along Fairview Strand, the dark clouds that had been looming from the west all day unleashed a freezing shower of sleety rain. Although the weather had threatened to make things unpleasant on a number of occasions, this was the first time over the fifty miles I had walked from the borders of Meath that it had actually carried out its threat, and it did so with a vengeance. I walked, quickly with head down, along the nondescript street until I reached the red-and-white painted brick front of Gaffney's public house. I turned in through the swing doors, shaking the raindrops off as I unslung my rucksack.

The inner bar was quiet after the noise of traffic outside. The place glowed with physical and psychological warmth, the yellow woods of the wall-panelling reflecting the glow of concealed light fittings. One man was sitting reading a paper at the narrow mahogany bar, while at a table in the back of the bar a young couple sat, he teasing her with comments about her taste in drinks, and she laughing softly at his jibes.

I ordered a glass of Guinness from a barman who materialised from an arched passage connecting the public bar, and admired the series of fine, framed half-models of nineteenth-century ship's hulls that decorated the walls. The pub has been called Gaffneys for nearly a hundred years; before that it was the Emerald Isle Inn, and before that again, in the early 1700s, it was the Big Gun Inn, renowned for its oysters, mussels and stewed cockles, all gleaned from the sea, which at that time lapped a shore twenty yards from the front door.

The barman, a Tipperary man, told me he had been working there since the early 1960s, and remembered that they used to do their own bottling on the premises — not only stout, but whiskeys and port. I have good reason to remember Gaffneys Invalid Port, as it was called, because many years ago I had an out-of-body experience there! At the time I was working in Merrion Square, and as part of a commission to design a church, I had a series of discussions with a sculptor regarding the design of the altar furniture. He lived in Howth, and we agreed one day on the phone that we would meet roughly half-way, and have lunch at a restaurant in Fairview.

Although I was not accustomed to taking a drink during the day, we had a gin and tonic before lunch, and somehow managed to dispose of a bottle of wine as we ate and discussed the project. After lunch, my sculptor friend invited me to take a glass of port in Gaffneys; he told me that it was one of the few places where the owners still kept a stock of their own vintage port at very reasonable prices, and it was something not to miss. I had never had port before, and it sounded most interesting. Gaffneys was only a few yards from where we had eaten, and within minutes I was sitting at the counter sipping that sweet, dark ruby liquor.

My sculptor friend seemed to know some of the customers, and I was introduced to a series of people, including a candle maker from Rathborne's, the renowned manufacturers. I bought a round, accepted a drink or two, and joined in the light-hearted conversation.

Time seemed to telescope, and at some stage I noticed that the conversation around me seemed to merge into a single, droning, meaningless sound, which gradually receded until it seemed to be coming from a long way off. I could only sit there on the stool, stunned by this phenomenon, which was accompanied by a heightened awareness of the minutest details of the cheerful faces around me. I had received no warning of the onset of inebriation; the journey from sobriety to footlessness seemed a momentary thing. One moment I was listening intently to a candle maker describing a particularly intricate operation in the candle-making process, the next I was out of it. I realised, with the last few sober brain cells I possessed, that I was very drunk!

What makes the occasion unforgettable is the fact that my eyes seemed to drift upwards, and I have a vivid memory of my sober self gazing down at the scene in Gaffneys from somewhere near the ceiling. Below, I could clearly see the balding pate of the sculptor, glass of port in hand, in animated conversation with the candle maker and two other men. I could also see myself, crouched on the stool at the bar as if it were a narrow ledge on a precipice, because those few sober brain cells that remained believed that if I were to step off the stool, I would simply fall to the floor. Meanwhile the barman briskly carried on his work polishing glasses, and moving up and down the bar.

No one seemed to notice my withdrawal from the conversation, and as my panic calmed a little, I began to take stock of the situation. It was as if I were two persons, the physical one, who was drunk, and the mental one, who found himself trapped in an inebriated body! I realised with horror that it was twenty past two; the pub would close at two thirty, and I would have to get off the stool, leave the pub, find my car and drive back across the Liffey to the office.

My sober persona decided that the first thing to do was to stop drinking. Apart from the half-finished glass I had been sipping, there were two more lined up on the counter; these would have to be sacrificed. Then I started to, surreptitiously, take deep breaths and exercise my legs experimentally under the stool. By the time the barman was calling 'time!' I had, through an enormous feat of concentration, psyched myself up to what I had to do, and I slid gingerly down from the stool and carefully followed my friend and his companions as they headed slowly for the door, still deep in conversation and apparently not noticing my condition.

The rest is a hazy memory; knowing I could not drive, I admitted my predicament to my friend, who immediately invited me home to Howth where we would have a sobering feed of salmon, after which he would bring me back to Fairview to collect my car. And so, five hours later I returned for my car, and left Gaffneys behind with a rueful knowledge of one good reason why what I had drunk there should be called 'invalid port'!

And so, twenty years later, I left Gaffneys again (the barman told me the invalid port was all gone) and, glad to find that the rain had ceased, headed across the road, and entered Fairview Park. They say that the rubble removed from O'Connell Street after the 1916 Rising was dumped here on the swampland that developed inland of the railway embankment, and that Fairview Park was laid out to top it off. It was a cold and windswept park when I walked through it, and I was relieved to reach the ugly tubular steel bridge that took me over the Tolka to the relative shelter of the houses of East Wall Road.

The Tolka rises near a place called Pelletstown on the fertile plains of County Meath, and reaches the East Wall after a course of nineteen miles. Here at East Wall Road it is at its best when the tide is in and swans cruise on its calm waters. I passed under the railway bridge as a diesel with the livery of Northern Ireland Railways clattered over. Some of the houses along East Wall Road, like their occupants, are old, in poor repair and grimly holding on; here and there, however, a bright, newly painted facade indicated that a young family had moved in. Some houses, having survived maybe seventy years with doubtful foundations on reclaimed land, are succumbing to the hammering of the traffic a few yards from their front doors, developing wavering rooflines, missing slates and crooked windows. As I walked, I was experiencing and suffering from the constant train of gargantuan articulated trucks that use East Wall Road, carrying much of the nine million tonnes of throughput shipping cargo that the port deals with every year.

Soon the Tolka veered away from the road, and I was confronted by the latest new expanse of reclaimed land, housing East Point Business Park, which turns the river towards the north. Since I could no longer follow the river, I continued down East Wall Road. On the south side of the road is an exceptionally fine stone-faced building with a columned entrance facade erected in the 1930s by Gallaghers, the tobacco company. Out of curiosity I looked up the entry for tobacco in a 1930s' encyclopaedia to see how the drug was regarded in those days when smoking was politically correct. It told me: 'Extensively used as a narcotic in chewing, snuff and smoking through cigars, pipes and cigarettes . . . Tobacco was brought to Europe by Francisco Fernandes, and was sent by Jean Nicot (whence Nicotine) to Catherine de Medici. . . . world production is about two million tons per annum.' There was no mention of the possible side-effects in those days; they were the halcyon days for the tobacco companies, a time when smoking was a part of most people's lives, and indeed it was *de rigueur* for the 1930s' equivalent to upwardly mobile yuppies to flaunt a cigarette and probably a silver cigarette case and tortoise-shell holder as fashion accessories. The Gallagher building was subsequently owned by Fry-Cadbury, the chocolatemakers, before being taken over in 1964 by paper manufacturers Wiggins Teape, one of those rare phenomena today — an old, long-established company that continues to thrive.

All the windows of the buildings further on were protected with steel grills or bars, suggesting that security was a problem hereabouts, but it had not prevented a couple of well-designed new IDA business centres from being established nearby.

Beyond Merchant's Road, a Coronation Street of red-bricked fronts, dense chimneys and television aerials, I was presented with a pleasant surprise. A painted sign, complete with a coat of arms bearing the words, 'Let your light shine', hung over the pavement in front of a nondescript brick building and announced the premises of John G. Rathborne, established in 1488. I remembered the candle maker of Gaffneys, but had thought the firm was long gone out of business; the freshness and quality of the sign belied this. I was intrigued by the longevity of the firm, so I went in to see if they had any short history of the establishment in a brochure.

I walked into the showrooms to be greeted by that unfamiliar but most pleasant aroma of beeswax. I looked briefly at the wall-to-wall display of candles of all shapes, sizes and colours and told a girl what I was looking for. She immediately introduced me to a man who was busily passing through, the sales manager of Rathborne's, Terry Roche.

'Would you like to have a look around the place?' he asked. 'I haven't long, but I'd be glad to show you around.'

I gladly took him up on his offer and he escorted me out across a yard to another building.

'There's an American guy here today,' he said, 'a photographer, and he's really overwhelmed with the place. He can't get over the antiquity of everything!'

He brought me into a large room filled with the cacophony of clicking, rattling machinery. A flexible tube hoovered up powdered paraffin wax from a great bin and delivered it to a machine that turned it into night-lights. A group of young women stood at the end of the assembly line doing the final packing. At the other end of the room, where a frame like a weird fruit tree suspended long tubers of beeswax, large church candles were made by the same technique of dipping the wick into a vat of beeswax that has been in use for centuries. The place was filled with an aroma which brought back memories of childhood power cuts and summer holidays in an old railway carriage on the Waterford coast.

'We used to have a hundred and twenty working here; now we have twenty-six, and we make more candles than we did then,' Terry told me, as he took me to a brick-walled shed lined with regularly spaced and ancient cast-iron machines. A man was working at a series of black bubbling cauldrons, in which two-foot square blocks of scarlet candle wax were being melted down. Melting wax dribbled over the sides of the cauldrons, forming fantastic stalactites and rivulets that pooled and became stalagmites on the floor. We made our way between the machines and I was introduced to Reggie Jackson, a small black American hung down with cameras, and Patrick, the man operating the machines. Terry told me that they did not use this equipment very often now because it was quite slow; the machines were about one hundred and fifty years old and moulded candles in the same way that had been done for centuries, by extruding heated wax into formes.

We were just in time to watch the process, and after making a few adjustments, Patrick began to turn a great handle shiny from years of use. Slowly, reels of white wick in a compartment at the bottom of the machine began to rotate, and the tips of two hundred red candles appeared from the top. Reggie went to work with great enthusiasm, using the colour and the patterns formed by the serried rows of emerging candles to the full; in his backgrounds he was including the intent face of Patrick, which reflected a warm glow from the candles as he strained at the rotating handle. In a few minutes the task was completed, the new candles were left to cool and Reggie could relax again. 'You know,' he said, turning to me, 'this is my first time in Ireland and I think everything is very magical here. Things seem to fall into place.'

In Rathborne's

He told me he had come to Ireland to photograph old crafts, and someone he met on the plane had recommended Rathborne's. 'And boy, am I glad! This is terrific!'

He was also giving workshops on the Chinese art of t'ai chi, and had been invited to give one in Portlaoise Prison. He had spent a day there, and had met Pat Kelly, an IRA man who had been 'repatriated' from an English prison because he had cancer. Reggie said, maybe a little surprised, that he found Kelly a very civilised and educated man, and they had talked for a long time. He said that Kelly had told him that while in jail in England he had been chained to his bed for eighteen hours a day; although chaining is common in the United States, Reggie was surprised that such a practice was carried on in Europe.

Reggie laughed and said he had not realised that the workshop he had agreed to give would be in a prison, and that he would spend a day there. '"Whadd are you doin' to me, man?" I said to the boss there. "They mightn't let me back into the United States now." I can get in prison very easy in the United States; we brothers don't have any trouble gettin' into prison,' he laughed.

He asked about Irish music and where he should go to hear it. I recommended County Clare for its music and set dancing. He said that he was interested in that because he thought that Irish music was one of the sources, another being African music, that developed into tap dancing in the States. I could have gone on talking to this interesting man for hours, but he had work to do, and I had a day's walk to end, so I bade Reggie and all at Rathborne's farewell and made my way out on to the street.

It was beginning to get dark now, and a cold breeze was blowing down East Wall Road, so I decided to bypass the port, and was relieved to benefit from the relative shelter as I rounded the corner and made my way down towards the toll bridge and the Liffey. Gaps in the tall wall surrounding the property of Dublin Port gave occasional glimpses of dry docks, tugboats and great buoys. Dublin Port is quite an empire unto itself, being the local authority over a huge area of Dublin's docks, much of which has been reclaimed from the sea over the last one and a half centuries. It even has its own police force, which has jurisdiction over the port area.

While Dublin would never have prospered without the access to and from the sea, this access was historically a major problem. The continued existence of the city beyond the Viking days is a small miracle because the two great sandbars that flanked the channel, through which the old Liffey entered the bay, have taken the lives of many hundreds of unfortunate sailors and swallowed up numerous ships. The entry to the Liffey was over a sandbar, allowing only two metres of water at low tide, which meant that many ships had to anchor in the bay until a favourable tide would allow them to proceed into Dublin. In the days of sail, ships were notoriously vulnerable to onshore gales, and although today's motor ships can travel against the wind, a sailing ship depended totally on its anchors to resist such winds, and they frequently failed, leaving the ship to be blown on to sandbanks or rocks.

It was the kind of powerful autonomy that the Harbour Board enjoys today that was responsible for the success of its predecessor, the Ballast Board, founded in 1707, which managed single-mindedly to procure and spend the stupendous sums of money required to carve a proper port out of a muddy swamp of an estuary. Hydrology was not even an infant science when a succession of engineers designed and had built constructions such as the Great North Wall and the Great South Wall, the latter in its time one of the largest projects of its kind in the world.

These dramatic physical interventions in the bay meant that by the 1880s the largest ships in the world, including *The Great Eastern*, were able to moor at the North Wall. There were side-effects also, such as the creation of new sandbanks and the silting up of areas beside the great walls. The Harbour Board took advantage of this by embarking on land reclamation on a huge scale, creating much new land projecting out into the bay.

I came to and passed the Point Depot, a great Victorian stone-built pile fronting on to the Liffey. The Point is a remarkable example of how an old building, designed for a particular purpose, can be successfully adapted to a radically different use. It started life in the 1850s as a repair shop for railway engines, but today the great hangar-like space accommodates huge audiences for musical performances. Most of its patrons pay astonishing amounts of money to sit in often draughty seats and see their musical heroes in the far distance, while listening to a poor quality amplification.

I had reached the Liffey, an important milestone in my journey along the County Dublin coast. The traffic was heavy as I scurried across the road out of the shelter of the Point Depot to the quayside and the river, just as a bitterly cold rain squall came from the west and blotted out the city. I had not time to get my coat out of my bag and on before I was drenched, and I turned and made my way damply towards O'Connell Street and home.

7

The Liffey to Sandymount

It was a hectic winter and spring for me, and almost seven months had elapsed before I was able to continue my coastal journey. On a bright and clear Friday morning in June, with a string of high cirrus paling the blue of the sky and filtering the sun, I was back again at the Point Depot on the north bank of the Liffey. I had about twenty-two miles to walk along the coast to reach the County Wicklow border, and I had decided to take three days to cover the distance, because I knew there would be a lot to see.

I was looking forward to these final miles; I was more familiar with the south coast of Dublin Bay than I was with the north, but I also knew that walking it would open up many new aspects. I asked a friend, James Doran, to accompany me on the first stretch south of the Liffey to Sandymount; he was born and reared in the area, and has many memories of recent 'rare ould times'. Since our walk would be a kind of pilgrimage to places where he had spent his youth, James brought along his twelve-year-old daughter, Emma, for the day.

We started in a leisurely way, strolling out across the East Link toll bridge. The bridge is the most recently constructed of the city's sixteen bridges, and carries over one hundred thousand vehicles a week. Its completion in 1984 saw the running of ferry-boats across the Liffey finally come to an end, a trade that had been in continuous operation for probably a thousand years. As with all cities founded on the banks of a river, passenger ferries formed an essential part in the workings and development of Dublin. Their importance and the need to control them is evidenced by the interest taken in them from the highest levels; a royal charter issued in the seventeenth century by Charles II laid down that ferries had to be available from one hour before sunrise to one hour after sunset, at a fixed charge of a halfpenny per passenger, and a penny per horse. As the bridges across the Liffey became more numerous, however, the ferries were forced further downstream, but it was not until the eve of the opening of the toll bridge in 1984 that the last ferry ran from Sir John Rogerson's Quay to East Wall Road. In the last year of operation, the ferries carried fifteen thousand passengers at a fare of ten pence per person. James told me that he had taken the ferry with his two sons on the last day of service, when all the trips were free, and a great crowd of Dubliners turned up to bid farewell to another aspect of old Dublin.

James talked of one old Liffey-side tradition that still clings on — the sport of skiff-rowing — and he pointed out, on the south quays, the headquarters of one of the remaining clubs, St Patrick's Skiff Club. There were no lightweight fibreglass or carbon fibre high-tech rockets of the water to be seen here. The boats used by St Patrick's Club are solid craft, clinker built in timber, and weighing near a ton, boats that require not just skill but brute strength to propel them through the water. A few of these craft were floating at moorings in front of the clubhouse near where the Dodder and the Grand Canal merge to join the Liffey.

Reaching the south side of the river, we turned east and walked beside what had once been the quay wall, but today it divides the new toll bridge road, built on land reclaimed from the river, from

York Road. We were now in Ringsend, where the people regard themselves not merely as Dubliners, but as a race apart. This is probably because, up to the seventeenth century the place was a mile-long, narrow and isolated peninsula extending out towards where the North Wall is today, with the eastern shore of Dublin Bay a mile further west, near the line of Upper Mount Street. The Gaelic word Rinn means a head or point of land, and it is to be supposed that 'Rinns End' was the tip of the point. For much of the eighteenth century Ringsend acted as the port of Dublin, and a fishing centre with a great reputation for oysters. A picturesque newspaper advertisement for October 1745 states:

> Poolbeg Oyster Fishery being taken this year by Messrs Bunit & Simpson, of Ringsend, they may be had fresh and in their purity at Mrs L'Swares at the Sign of the Good Woman in Ringsend aforesaid.

Ringsend must have deteriorated badly over the following sixty years, because a description dating from 1816 states:

> On approaching the town you pass through a vile, filthy and disgraceful-looking village called 'Ringsend'.

One wonders what the people of Ringsend did to this reporter to bring out such bile!

James pointed out an unusual characteristic of the tightly packed terrace of houses in a street called Pembroke Cottages, built in 1893. They had front doors that opened out, an unusual if not unique feature, the reason for which I cannot imagine. James said that they were called locally the Protestant Cottages because of this strange phenomenon! The name Pembroke refers to the Pembroke Estates, the vast tracts of south Dublin land owned originally by the Fitzwilliam family of Merrion, which came into the possession of George Augustus, eleventh Earl of Pembroke, in 1816. The tomb of the original and first Earl of Pembroke, known as Richard de Clare or Strongbow, can be found in Christ Church Cathedral, a couple of miles upriver.

In the distance now, the two red-and-white striped chimneys of the ESB power station at the Pigeon House beckoned at the end of a long straight road, lined with a terrace of forty-four brick-fronted cottages, like a lesson in perspective. The cottages were of modest design, but, in true Victorian fashion, the designer had introduced a little piece of delight by siting at the western gable end of the terrace a fine granite-pinnacled brick drinking fountain, now unfortunately defunct. The cottages in recent years have all grown a tiny porch on to their facades, courtesy of the developers of the toll bridge, to reduce the noise and pollution caused by the increase in traffic.

We took our life in our hands to dart across the busy toll road to the new quay wall and view the river. A rich variety of craft lay moored and reflected in the calm waters of the Liffey: yachts, motor launches, old-fashioned rowing boats, and even a pookan, the younger sister of the Galway hooker, often used for fishing in inland waters. A heron was perching on the stern of a sailing skiff as if skippering it, like a character in a children's book; all that was needed was for the bird to be wearing a nautical cap and smoking a corn-cob pipe for the picture to be complete.

Near the Stella Maris boat club, the main opposition for the boys of St Patrick's Skiff Club, a spur from Ringsend Park reaches the road. James pointed out a long straight path that forms the eastern boundary of the park and which was known when he was a child as the Main Drain, probably because the primary sewer for the south city ran under it to the treatment works further east. Ringsend's sewage treatment works have been performing a major and essential service for the city of Dublin since the 1880s. The treatment plant for the south city was established in Ringsend at that time, and today it handles a mind-boggling three hundred and twenty-three million gallons of the unmentionable per day, a mere seventeen thousand litres per second!

One building along this roadside harks back to a time when the open sea was much nearer than it is today. The Ringsend coastguard station, a terrace of granite-fronted houses terminating in a two-storey tower with a pyramidic roof and mock machicolations, was built when this was the eastern point of Ringsend, surrounded on three side by the waters of the bay.

As we progressed eastwards, we found ourselves in a strange industrial zone, a place of cargo containers and high fences, in the midst of which cowered a forgotten terrace of red-brick houses. On a garbage-strewn street two small boys were noisily playing football with an empty beer-can. Nearby stood the boarded-up headquarters of the 1st Port Sea Scouts, the first Scout troop established in Ireland by Robert Baden-Powell, founder of the Boy Scouts and Girl Guides movement. Many of the wire-enclosed container compounds were derelict and covered in jungles of unusually tall plants that had forced their way up through the macadam and concrete pavings. Elsewhere these plants would have been regarded as weeds and would have been purged before they had managed to reach any size, but here, un-preyed upon by gardener or road cleaner, they reached gloriously skywards, stretching to their full potential. Their thriving is likely to generate a significant increase in the local population of insects and seed-eating birds; as evidence of this, Emma, who had been walking ahead, called to us to come and see a colourful collection of ladybirds, clustered like red blossoms on the top of a bright green plant.

We were passing through a newly developing wilderness — a phenomenon common to all modern cities and brought about by rapid industrial progress, followed by dereliction and neglect; much of the land we were walking upon had been reclaimed from the sea at great expense and had been intensively used as part of port operations until the 1970s, when containerisation had changed the way the port worked. Now acres of semi-disused land, scattered with rusting sheds and broken-down machinery, lay all around; only the fencing protecting these areas was being kept in good order, to prevent access by squatters or a travelling community looking for somewhere to live. When all the jungles and deserts of the world have been explored, tamed and turned into tourist venues, places like this, where nature has reasserted itself, may provide new challenges. Adventurous trekkers will tackle the disused and overgrown cores of the cities, crossing on foot the urban jungles, braving chemical poisoning and predators, both human and animal!

The road looped around to rejoin the Pigeon House Road, and we passed a dilapidated grouping of tin sheds which had started life as St Mary's Smallpox Hospital, run by the Sisters of Charity. It was located here early in the twentieth century, close to the port but away from the city, to deal with an expected epidemic of the disease which never occurred. Eventually the buildings became part of the country-wide scheme established by Health Minister Noël Browne in the early 1950s to treat and eradicate tuberculosis.

Great clumps of valerian and hawk-bit colourfully decorated the old stone wall beside the road, and Emma, leaning over it, beckoned us to look down into the waters of a short canal-like stretch of water flowing on the far side. She pointed into the water and excitedly counted a shoal of large mullet that were cruising shark-like up and down, creating ripples and wakes on the calm surface, giving me another glimpse of a rich wildlife in a place where I least expected it.

The road now led us directly towards the tall red-and-white striped chimneys of the Ringsend Power Station, and off to the left a brief view of the Hill of Howth came into sight across Dublin Bay, beyond the Bull Wall. Suddenly we were assailed by a noxious smell, and we realised that we were passing the sewage settlement tanks, the least pleasant of Ringsend's tourist attractions. James and I laughed at Emma's face of utter disgust, but we all held our noses and crossed to the far side of the road — as if a few yards would make any difference! The miasma had receded somewhat by the time we reached the remains of the great limestone gateway to the Pigeon House Fort.

About 1760, a watch-house and store were built near here and when a John Pidgeon was employed by the port authority as a caretaker, he moved into the watch house with his family. Pidgeon seems to have been something of an entrepreneur, because after

Old gateway

the completion of the great South Wall, he is to be found providing refreshments to passengers who were embarking or disembarking from the mail packet boat moored at the wall and, with his son, providing pleasure trips by boat to Ringsend and back. The watch-house soon became known as Pidgeon's House, and by the middle of the nineteenth century the whole area was known as The Pigeon House.

The single stone gate pier here is one of the few remains of the

Pigeon House Fort, built after the last turbulent years of the eighteenth century for the defence of the port, and once a substantial fortified establishment. It was also used to provide a secure repository for bullion, state papers and other valuables during times of disturbance, a place from where they could be easily shipped to England should matters in Ireland get out of control. Gun revetments, which originally looked out over and controlled the waters of the Liffey, today oversee reclaimed land carpeted in yellow Lady's Lace; and buddleias, willows, elders and a lone laburnum sprout colourfully where redcoats once paraded.

To the north-east, beyond where the old, disused power station stands, another battery of the fort was used to deter Daniel O'Connell from holding one of his monster meetings at Clontarf in October 1843. During that year the increasingly militant O'Connell had addressed a series of public gatherings all around the country, whipping up support for the repeal of the Act of Union. Great crowds of supporters attended these meetings, which were held in historically significant locations; the monster meeting on the Hill of Tara is said to have attracted a quarter of a million people. The final demonstration was to have been on Conquer Hill, in Clontarf, sacred in the Irish tradition as the location of the Battle of Clontarf where Brian Boru defeated the foreigners. The British Prime Minister, Sir Robert Peel, could see that full-scale rebellion was in the offing, and the meeting was banned. Troops surrounded Conquer Hill, warships cruised up and down Dublin Bay, and the Pigeon House batteries were turned on the shore; O'Connell called off the meeting, signalling the beginning of the end for his Repeal Movement. Before the month was out, O'Connell had been arrested for conspiracy and the following year he was committed to a year's imprisonment.

At the gates of the power station, one of the cannon that once guarded the entry to Dublin port is mounted on its wooden trestle, embossed with the date 1770, a crown, and the motif of the Royal Ordnance Factory. Looking at this rather primitive piece of ordnance, it is hard to believe how far the art of killing has advanced since the time when this crude weapon was a state-of-the-art artillery piece, a mere two hundred years ago. Within the ESB compound, like something from the set of a science-fiction movie, the rust-stained, disused power station towers over a grey bow-fronted building that was once the Pigeon House Hotel, built about 1793.

The road veers around to the south to reach the edge of the sands that sweep all the way to the shore at Sandymount. There is a little beach here, overlooking what James called the Cockle Lake. When I mentioned that I had thought that Cockle Lake was near Clontarf, he replied, like a true southsider, that anything worthwhile that existed on the north side had to be repeated on the south side!

A wonderful panorama was now laid out before us: a vast flat landscape of sands with interspersed patches of silver reflecting water stretched to the south and east, where in the far distance a line of white surf could be seen, and as far and all as it was away, the sound of its continuous sibilant rushing could be heard. A few groups were digging for lugworms out on the sands; perhaps before long they would be standing on the stony beaches of Wicklow or north Wexford, casting their harvest of these colourful creatures into the surf of a rising tide to catch sea bass.

The low-lying peninsula of reclaimed land we had been following eastwards had narrowed down now to almost three hundred yards, as the road skirted around the Ringsend Power Station with its towering pair of chimneys. The port authority had planted a border of escallonia and American daisies along this wind-swept and exposed road, and they were thriving remarkably well in thick, ground-hugging clumps. As we passed the power station, with the air full of lark song, the peninsula ended at a little beach, and the South Wall, exposed finally to its original width, stretched into the distance to the bulbous, red Poolbeg lighthouse. One has to stand upon it to fully comprehend what vision and confidence was involved in the conception of such a measure, and what an enormous undertaking was its construction in the 1730s. I believe that without that vision and confidence, Dublin port would never have developed as it did, and consequently the capital and indeed the country would not have developed as it has.

We stopped a while at the little beach for some refreshments, sitting on the rocks and absorbing the sun and air. The weather had been very kind, and rather than deteriorating, as had been promised by the benighted weather forecasters, it had improved, a strong breeze shifting scudding cloudlets away from the sun.

It was good to get going again, out along the wall, a twelve-feet-wide matrix of coursed blocks of mica-glistening granite that had weathered more than two hundred and thirty winters. As we walked, the pilot boat outpaced us, splashing its way out the deep channel to the north like a speed boat to service the queue of ships entering the outer bay. Only yards away a heavily laden tanker, with the name *Borgstellar Berg* emblazoned on its spray-drenched bows, rumbled rhythmically in towards the Liffey, flag flapping at its stern. The purpose of the South Wall is clear to see here, with large ships cruising in and out close to the northern side, while on the south side dry sands stretch into the distance, sands that are covered by only shallow waters even at high tide.

As we neared the Poolbeg lighthouse, we came to a little flat-roofed building beside a south-facing walled enclosure with seats, from which steps led down to the waters of the bay. This was the clubhouse and changing room of the Half-Moon Swimming Club, founded in 1898. The name 'Half Moon', it is thought, harks back to when there was a battery of cannon established here in 1793, and probably refers to a half-circle gun emplacement. In those days heavy guns could not be swivelled, so, to ensure hits on a moving target, such as a ship moving towards the Liffey, a number of guns, with different fields of fire, had to be used. The walls of the hollow-sounding, windowless clubhouse were decorated with photographs of smiling male bathers braving winter weather, and records of air and water temperatures; for instance on 19 December 1993 the water temperature was forty-two degrees Fahrenheit, the air temperature was the same, and the conditions bright and windy.

The Poolbeg lighthouse

The impressive bulk of the lighthouse, so long our distant goal, finally loomed over us as we reached the end of the South Wall. It is a magical experience to stand facing the open sea with the lighthouse at your back. You stand as if on the tips of the waves in the middle of Dublin Bay, with an almost three-hundred-and-sixty-degree panorama of sky, sea and shore all about you. To the south Killiney Hill edges its way down to the sea, and Dalkey Island stands aloof off the coast. The far-off shore of the bay, picturesquely scattered with buildings and trees, sweeps past Dun Laoghaire reaching westwards to Sandymount, with the Dublin Mountains providing a great rolling backdrop. To the north lies the great whale-back of Howth, tenuously linked to the dense clusters of cranes and masts of Dublin Port by a low-lying neck of land.

The Poolbeg lighthouse was completed in 1767 and originally had an external staircase of granite steps cantilevered from the walls, giving access to the top, which was somewhat lower than it is today. The enormous blocks of stone, encrusted with barnacles and seaweed, which radiate out from the base of the tower, are the top of the great pile of such stones that the lighthouse is founded upon.

After sitting a while in the shelter of the lighthouse, we started back inland. A lone member of the Half-Moon Club was sprawled out on a seat enjoying the sun; he must not have been wearing a bathing suit because he tugged a towel across his waist as we passed. The tide was rising, encroaching slowly but steadily across the sands to our left. Keeping ahead of it was a man dressed in dungarees and wellington boots, a bucket in one hand and a stick with a hook on it in the other, with which he seemed to be re-arranging strands of seaweed on the boulders along the edge of the wall. We were puzzled; he did not seem to be picking mussels, which although numerous on the rocks, were very small, nor did he seem to be picking periwinkles. James suggested light-heartedly that the man was tidying up the seaweed.

I asked him if he minded my enquiring about what he was doing.

'I'm looking for a few peeler crabs,' he said, and indicated with his hooked stick how he was turning over fronds of seaweed to reveal the wildlife underneath. He stooped, and picking up a small crab, demonstrated that it was actually soft.

Emma stood between us and gazed, fascinated, as he pulled a leg off and then discarded the crab.

'Are they edible?' I enquired.

'Yeh, well, you could eat them, but I collect them for bait. You see, they've shed their old shells and the new shell that's forming is still soft.'

'What fish would you catch with them?' James asked.

'Most fish'll take them, I think.' He turned over more seaweed, and repeated the process of picking up crabs, tugging off a leg, and tossing them aside. I was horrified to see that, at this rate, most of the crabs in Dublin Bay would be minus a leg, and had to ask, 'But why do you pull off their legs?'

He picked up another and showed me that when he removed a leg, a long slip of tendon remained. He explained that a green or red tendon indicated it was a peeler, a young crab just ideal for using as bait.

'A lot of them are not big enough to harvest yet, and I leave them off, they're next year's supply! Some of them are carrying, eh, youngsters in their purse. They're females, and we don't take those. A he-crab like this, we call him a jack.'

He plucked yet another leg and said, 'See, this is a peeler.' He pointed out the bright green colour of the exposed tendon. We oohed and aahed our understanding as he lobbed it into his bucket. Thanking him for enlightening us, we headed across the sands for Ringsend Park.

The lugworm diggers had gone, leaving little clear pools and heaps of sand after them. A lone golfer practising his drive paused as a strange mirage shimmering over the sands between us and Sandymount turned into a pair of horses and riders. We crunched along over cockle- and razor-shells until we reached the recently established coastline of Irishtown Nature Park. We climbed up a low cliff of old concrete telegraph poles, bricks and boulders and followed a tree-bark-covered path to the south. The air was full of perfume from the blossoms of the thick grasses and herbs that covered the man-made hill and, rounding a corner, we marvelled at the density of yellow-flowered oil-seed rape that covered the south-facing slopes, like a picture from Provence.

We passed through Seán Moore Park, commemorating a 1960s' Lord Mayor of Dublin, near where the Waxies' Dargle used to be held. In the eighteenth century the well-off citizens of Dublin used take open coaches out to Bray in the summer, where they would enjoy themselves picnicking on the shaded banks of the river Dargle. The cobblers of the city could not afford to travel so far for their annual outing; instead, they had their picnics on the strand near here, a place that became known both through song and story as the Waxies' Dargle.

If we had arrived at Beach Road some three hundred years earlier, it would have been difficult to avoid dropping in to a renowned public house and inn called The Conniving House, that stood near Seafort Avenue. It was a thatched building overlooking the shore, and boasted, according to a contemporary account by Thomas Amory, 'the finest fish at all times, and in season, green peas and all the most excellent vegetables . . . the ale here was always extra-ordinary, and everything the best'. Amory went on to extol the music to be enjoyed in the evenings, performed by 'the famous Larry Grogan, who played on the bagpipes extremely well; dear John Lattin, matchless on the fiddle . . . the most agreeable of companions'. The nearest thing to the Conniving House available in today's Sandymount is O'Reilly's public house, a good place to end a day's walk, and we slipped into its dark-panelled, cosy lounge and took our ease, surrounded by the pleasant murmur of relaxed conversations.

8

Sandymount to Sandycove

I resumed my odyssey the following day at Beach Road in Sandymount. At the time in the early eighteenth century when the Conniving House was enjoying the patronage of the academic staff and students of Trinity College, Sandymount had not yet come into being. The area consisted of a marshland separated from the sea by a rabbit warren, and, when in the 1730s it was found that the underlying clays were suitable for brick-making, the area was exploited by the landowners to supply the increasing need for building materials in an expanding Dublin. The gathering of dwellings used by the brick-makers became known by the 1760s as Brickfield Town. It is probable that the removal of large volumes of material led to the area becoming inundated at high tides, which may have been why Lord Fitzwilliam had a protective sea-wall built from Ringsend to Merrion, thus establishing the present shoreline.

The Fitzwilliam family also had ambitious plans to reclaim the vast tract of shore between the South Wall and Booterstown, and a number of unsuccessful attempts were made to get government approval and financial aid for the project, the last in the 1870s.

Over the years a series of circumstances led to the transformation of the modest brick-makers' village into the

141

emerging middle-class suburb of Sandymount; contributing factors were the population explosion in Dublin in the later eighteenth century, pollution in the city brought about by the burgeoning factories and workshops, and the new-found popularity of 'watering places'.

I climbed down to the sands of Sandymount Strand and strode out briskly along the shore, which swept around towards the spires of Dun Laoghaire about four miles away. The tide was far out, glittering in the morning sun between Dun Laoghaire pier and the Hill of Howth, leaving slivers of glistening silver ponds across the expanse of dark sands that remained; I could have been Joyce's Stephen Dedalus, 'walking into eternity on Sandymount Strand'. My intention was to get as far as I could that day along the sands before the incoming tide drove me ashore. The only complication I could foresee was the possible existence of streams entering the sea, which might make my passage damp in places.

A pair of horses — they may have been the same pair I had noticed the day before — were being put through their paces far out towards the Poolbeg, and, in the morning brightness and the exaggerated perspective of the bay, a mirage-like man walking his dog near the tideline looked like a giant beside a huge, ungainly car-transporter that was moored offshore, awaiting a pilot to guide it upriver.

The houses on Strand Road facing out on to the bay display little ostentation and make for a rich and colourful mixture of styles, all of a comfortable scale. One of them belongs to Ruairi Quinn, Labour Party leader and a former Minister for Finance, and I was reminded that Sandymount had been home to a number of the prominent politicians of modern Ireland, including Eamon de Valera and two Fine Gael taoisigh, John A. Costello and Garret FitzGerald, in addition to Seán MacEntee and Noël Browne.

Sandymount's Martello tower, the first I had come across since

Howth, has long been a symbol of Sandymount Strand. It seemed to have been recently turned into a restaurant, and less than successfully extended, the lack of quality in the workmanship and materials in stark contrast to the original. About fifty yards offshore, the old swimming baths, which once terminated a Victorian cast-iron pier, rose forlornly from the sands. The old whitewash was streaked green with seaweed, bearing a message that proclaimed 'Some men see things as they are, and ask why; I see things as they might be, and ask why not.' This strand was, for almost two hundred years, a hugely popular summer recreation place, but the use of the far shore at Irishtown as the tip-head for Dublin's garbage has changed all that. The future is good, however, because this part of the bay is now recovering well, and the houses facing out towards Howth along the shore here are bound to increase considerably in value.

The first stream I encountered was just before the Merrion Gates, but it was easy to hop over it. Beyond there was a bit of a swamp, but I was able to clamber along the sloped bottom of the sea wall to bypass it. A little further on I found a cove-like beach, backed on to by a couple of houses. On the wall at the rear of one of the houses two plaques were mounted with messages that mixed sadness and joy. One was only partially readable, and asked passers-by to tread softly there, noting that the ashes of a young woman, who had died at the age of twenty-nine were 'cast on the tide near this house, where she lived and loved, February 1986'. The other commemorated 'Joan F. Sharp, aged eighty-three, wife, mother, friend, who for twenty-five years made this house happy, August 1989'.

At the Merrion Gates the railway emerges on to the shore. Originally called the Dublin to Kingstown Railway when it was completed in 1834, it was the first passenger-carrying railway to be built in Ireland, and it transformed the south coast of Dublin Bay.

It is difficult today to appreciate the magnitude of the leap forward in communications that the advent of the railway brought in 1834. The idea of transporting materials on rails was not new. Miners in northern Germany had developed the use of wooden tracks to ease the movement of heavily laden wooden-wheeled ore carts in the Middle Ages. Steam power was not new either; Archimedes recognised its potential in the third century before Christ, and Leonardo da Vinci had toyed with a wheel turned by steam jets in the sixteenth century. While steam-driven machinery of many types had become common by the end of the eighteenth century, success in the use of steam to propel vehicles was elusive. The French Ministry of War peremptorily rejected development of a three-wheeled steam-driven gun carriage in 1769 because it had broken down after just fifteen minutes. In England an engineer called William Murdock constructed and tested a steam-driven road vehicle in 1784, but did not pursue the idea because the local vicar and people looked upon it as a manifestation of the devil himself! Finally, real progress began to be made when the first steam-driven ship had its maiden voyage on the Seine in 1803, and the following year the first steam locomotive to run on rails went to work at Merthyr Tydfil in Wales, pulling wagons of iron ore. In 1807, these remarkably far-sighted comments about the potential of steam power appeared in the *New York Mirror*: 'Where will this steam lead? Up to now man has been tied to his place like an oyster or a tree. Steam to a much more remarkable degree than any other previous development will alter the conditions of life for humanity. It will decrease the extent of the globe.'

It was the large-scale passenger-carrying possibilities that really made the railways such a major force for social change, and when the Darlington to Stockton Railway, engineered by George Stephenson and his son Robert, began operation in 1826 using passenger carriages, the Railway Age had well and truly dawned.

The new technology spread across the world at a phenomenal rate; the United States had its first railway in 1830, Canada in 1831, and France's first line was opened in 1833.

Ireland, as an important part of the United Kingdom, did not have to wait long for the introduction of railway technology; an act was passed in 1831 clearing the way for a line between Dublin and Kingstown, as Dun Laoghaire was then called, and after seeking the advice of eminent engineers such as Alexander Nimmo, Thomas Telford and George Stephenson, Charles Vignoles completed the plans for the system, and construction began in 1833.

There was widespread enthusiasm for the project, and even the contemporary magazine *The Dublin Penny Journal*, which concerned itself so much with Ireland's past, carried a number of laudatory articles describing the new railway, and suggesting that it could become instrumental in abating many of the 'evils' besetting Ireland, from absentee landlordism to low wages. Apart from dealing with the philosophical aspects of this advent of the railway, one issue of the enlightened periodical included a detailed technical description of the workings of the locomotive to be used on the new line.

The project was not carried out without opposition, however. At the Dublin end, the intention of having the terminus within 'a very short distance of the very centre of Dublin business' was thwarted by 'vague fears . . . and misrepresentations', and the 'Entrance Station' had to be located at Westland Row. In Dun Laoghaire the residents strongly opposed the 'proposed desecration of their town by this vulgar and demonic mode of conveyance', and prevented the line coming further than the beginning of the West Pier.

Two powerful landlords, Lord Cloncurry and Sir Harcourt Lees, owned lands and residences at Blackrock which would be cut off from the shore by the proposed railway line, and they provided serious opposition to the project. Substantial cash compensation, together with the construction of an elaborate twin-towered foot-bridge from Lord Cloncurry's land to the shore, took care of the opposition. It is clear that the investors were so convinced that the railway would bring huge financial rewards that no expense was spared, and in spite of all the difficulties that would naturally attend such a pioneering, radical proposal, this fact and the incisiveness of the main contractor, William Dargan, enabled Ireland's first rail line to open for business in December 1834. It carried an astonishing five thousand passengers on the first day of operation.

Beyond the Merrion Gates I walked along the great stone embankment which, when the railway was first built, ran straight out across the sands for almost a mile and a half. For a few hundred yards I seemed to be passing through a place where rubbish collects; the sand and gravel underfoot displayed a mixture of plastic bags, disposable nappies, and an abundance of whelks and spindle shells of all sizes. I picked a few examples and stuffed them into my bag, and then came across a huge whelk with flared flanges at the opening. I could not resist it and I managed to pack it away also. It sits on my desk as I write, still leaking fine white sand, and when I hold it to my ear it puts me in touch with faraway oceans.

Looking back, I could see that the chimneys of the Ringsend Power Station were finally receding into the distance, and the hill of yellow rape in Irishtown Park was catching the sun and reflecting it gloriously over the pools of Sandymount Strand.

A long green DART whined by, as if suspended from its overhead wires, and slowed to stop at Booterstown Station. I found a flight of steps that took me up on to the wall of the embankment, and crossed over a foot-bridge into the station. Since this section of the railway was built out across the sand flats, much of the area between the embankment and the original shore has been reclaimed, but here at Booterstown the station and its car park bisect a piece of marsh left much to its own devices since the 1830s, a place which has become a nature reserve. Marsh grasses with clumps of bird's foot trefoil cover the area west of the car park, and are separated from the railway embankment — its face a riot of pink and white valerian — by a long, narrow pond.

From the car park I watched a heron standing at the margins of the pond, within yards of the railway, ignoring the DART traffic. Mallards were taking off and landing continuously, and a female anxiously led six tiny chicks away from me through the marsh grasses and into the water. A wren sitting in an elder at the margin was emitting a stream of brittle invective at me from his long needle-like beak as I walked eastwards into the other side of the park. Here I passed a larger pond, disturbing two shelducks; this stretch of water is, I am told, a great place to see teal, lapwings and redshanks in winter-time. As I

Shelducks

walked I became aware for the first time of the constant traffic streaming along the Rock Road, overlooked by the great bulky monolith of the First National Building Society offices.

After a few minutes a bank of trees cloaked the view of the road, and I came upon a Travellers' encampment. A few caravans and sheds were sheltered in the trees, as if they had always been there. An elderly woman came out of one and wished me good morning.

I asked her where I could get back down on to the shore.

'You can get down further on,' she said with a touch of a Northern accent. 'There's a bridge goin' across. Isn't it a beautiful mornin', thank God?'

I agreed and said, 'You've a grand quiet spot here.'

'It's grand and sunny, and mild near the sea, if they'd only build the site. I don't know what they're doin'. They gave us the bin there so we can keep the place clean; they gave us the container, and they gave us toilets, but they won't give us water.'

'How do you manage, then?'

'Aw, it's terrible, aw, it's very awkward. The College, ye know Blackrock College, we haves to go up the yard an' bring the water down by churn. I don't know why they won't let us have a supply; it's terrible, and it's a very important thing, to clean your things, your utensils, yourself. The churn is the only thing we have. I went up to the Council a week ago, but I couldn't see any of the head men, you know. I was told by someone in there that they were goin' to put water in here twelve months ago. Forty-five, nearly fifty years I been here. I sent my children to school to Haddington Road out of it.'

I was surprised at the length of time, and asked her if she had travelled in between.

'No, we didn't, because we were sending the children to school. I had six boys. If you could help at all it would be great. Like, we love this place, but the thing is, the water. One of the people down there was tellin' me it should have been put in twelve months ago. I got a nun last week to write a letter; water is the whole thing.'

She asked me if I was a newspaperman. I told her I was writing about the Dublin coast, and had come from the border of County Meath.

'Sure we're next-door neighbours,' she said, misunderstanding me. 'I'm from Westmeath. That's where I was born, but I hardly ever go down there.'

I asked her if she had travelled a lot in her life.

'Mostly the North — the six counties. I married a man from Kildare, but he was mostly in the North; he was brought up there. He'll be home soon; I'd better get his dinner!'

She thanked me for listening to her complaints and, wishing

me well and God Bless, climbed back inside the caravan. I passed by two Portaloos, and then left the shady grove of trees and walked out into the noise of the traffic.

The Martello tower, like the previous one at Sandymount, had elaborate bulbous corbels under the parapet, and was much more decorative than the towers further north. Behind the tower I crossed a bridge over the railway to reach the sandy shore again.

The copper-clad roof of the Blackrock Clinic stood above the roofs of the older buildings inland. I wondered at the appropriateness of the motif of the medical profession, two snakes racing each other up a pole, that was mounted at the highest point of the roof. Ahead, projecting out from the embankment, were the old Blackrock Baths. There was a public bathing place here as early as the 1790s, and when the railway was built, the railway company constructed new baths for male and female bathers. Storms washed these away in 1886, and the following year they were rebuilt by the local authority in 'concrete cement', together with the promenade and seating that still exist.

As I walked briskly along the sands, a little turnstone ran along in front of me, his legs a blur, until he gave up and flitted ahead to land at the edge of the imperceptibly rising tide. Sea water was encroaching on the sands and merging, ripple by ripple, with the still pools. I was surprised to see that the leading edge of the sea was alive with a myriad tiny fish, a sign that the much-talked-about pollution of the water in this area is not as serious as might be thought.

Closer to the Blackrock Baths, it became clear that my time on the foreshore was going to be limited. I could see that, while there were expanses of sand as yet untouched by the rising tide, there were areas where shallow inlets brought water right in to the rocks. Beyond the baths I was amazed to see, straddling the railway line, the twin Italianate towers of Lord Cloncurry's bridge which had given him access to the shore one hundred and sixty years before.

Readers of this narrative who use the DART line will be familiar with this relic of a bygone age, but while I had seen contemporary drawings of the elaborate piece of architecture, I had assumed that it had, along with Cloncurry's summer-house, long since succumbed to progress. The summer residence was called 'Maritimo', and it was one of the three big houses on the Blackrock coast in the early nineteenth century; with the others, 'Neptune', owned by Lord Clonmel, and 'Blackrock', owned by Sir Harcourt Lees, it had a reputation for summer garden parties and all-night balls. 'Maritimo' lasted, surrounded by its gardens on the rising ground above the railway line, until it was demolished in 1970 and replaced by a block of flats. The tower bridge, more elaborate than the house itself, has stood the passage of time very well, although the windows have long been blocked up, and the granite ball finials that topped the towers have disappeared.

Tea-house

The rising tide drove me on to the railway embankment and I had to hop, skip and jump to cross a stream emitting from a culvert, before reaching another perk that local landowners had managed to wrest from the railway company. *The Dublin Penny Journal* of the period referred to the railway company erecting near here, in addition to the bridge, 'beautiful granite pavilions'. A few minutes after passing Lord Cloncurry's bridge, I came upon a tiny tea-house or bathing chalet, in the form of a tall-pedimented Doric-columned Roman temple, half hidden by bushes and overlooking the bay.

It was at about this point that I could see that the geology of the coast was undergoing a dramatic change. The limestone of the Dublin basin, after a brief appearance on the surface to give Blackrock its name, yields way further east to the northern extremity of the Wicklow granite field, the most extensive area of surface granite in the British Isles. The railway had to be tunnelled for a short distance through the rock, which assumes a very ragged, rough surface where it is exposed at the shore, encrusted with barnacles and mussels, concealing deep clear pools jewelled by bright red sea anemones. Here, perched on top of the rocks and surrounded by clusters of sea-pinks, I found the remains of yet another tea-house, a six-sided brick building with gothic windows.

The sea had now covered the sands ahead, seeing off a flock of oyster-catchers which had gathered there and leaving a lone heron poised, 'ankle' deep, stalking prey. I followed the railway embankment to Seapoint, and watched as the new HSS car ferry made its way into Dun Laoghaire Harbour, looking more like a giant train than a ship. As I reached the bathing place at Seapoint, the wake of the great vessel, consisting of numerous small breakers, was crashing on to the shore. There is another Martello tower here, and I can remember in the 1960s entering its cavernous, clammy and cool interior in summer-time to buy ice creams. A sign on the wall asks that, in the interests of hygiene, people should please refrain from walking dogs in this area, but, looking along the promenade ahead, I could see at least a dozen people doing just that.

Ahead now, a building that might have been a modern church, topped by a set of pyramidic roofs, rose from a headland of reclaimed land at Salthill. I was intrigued as to why a church should be built in such a place, and was not a little amazed to find when I got closer that this exotic temple housed the West Pier Pumping Station! Beautifully designed and finished in a combination of polished limestone and granite, the building stands in an expansive sea of stone cobbles, and the Sewer Gods hummed gently as I passed by, and reached Dun Laoghaire's West Pier.

About the time that the construction work began on the ill-fated packet station at Howth, a series of shipwrecks occurred in Dublin Bay, culminating in a two-ship disaster in 1807. In November of that year a storm drove the packet ship *HMS Prince of Wales*, and a troop transport, *The Rochdale*, on to the south coast of Dublin Bay, with a loss of three hundred and eighty lives. A petition was presented to the Lord Lieutenant of Ireland requesting his support for the construction of a safe 'asylum' or haven in Dublin Bay, where shipping, delayed by the tides from entering the port, could shelter during storms. It is probable that, behind this petition, there was also a continuance of the struggle to have the packet station, so recently lost to Howth, re-established on the south coast of Dublin Bay. In fact, by 1811, the beginnings of silting in the new harbour at Howth signalled that this relocation would be necessary before long.

Lobbying went on for some years, but practical advances were delayed by the Napoleonic Wars. By 1814, however, those with commonage rights on Dalkey Hill, from where much of the stone used to build the South Wall had been quarried, had agreed to donate the stone to build the harbour without charge. The funding was eventually made available, and the foundation stone was laid by Earl Whitworth, the Lord Lieutenant, in 1817. By the time this happened, what had begun as a project for a safe haven in a storm had expanded to become one of the finest man-made harbours in the world, with piers enclosing two hundred and fifty-one acres of water, at a cost, by the time the major works were completed in the 1860s, of one million pounds.

The resultant harbour did indeed provide safety for the increasing shipping using Dublin port; by as early as 1824 it is said that a total of three thousand, three hundred and fifty-one vessels had taken shelter there. Elaborate arrangements were made to welcome King George IV, who was to arrive at the harbour to begin a royal visit to Ireland in 1821, but for some reason he landed at Howth. He did, however, use Dun Laoghaire a month later for his departure from Ireland, renaming the place 'Kingstown' and the new harbour 'The Royal Harbour of George IV' before sailing home on board an early paddle steamer, renamed *Royal Sovereign* to commemorate the voyage. By the mid 1820s, it became impossible to keep Howth Harbour economically dredged, and Kingstown became Ireland's main mail and passenger terminus for England.

The West Pier is massive and long, the grass growing down the middle providing a strange rural touch. The nineteenth-century coastguard station near the pier is a particularly fine example; the same basic plan that is used around the coast of Ireland has been followed, but in this case the building was grander in every way than any I had previously seen. The tower and the captain's quarters were elaborately conceived, with granite facing and red brick window surrounds. The building is now owned by the Commissioners of Irish Lights, and behind it, a great and colourful conglomeration of buoys, big and small, some with bells, others with radar reflectors, was arrayed on the pier, all brightly reflecting the sunshine.

I walked past a long queue of cars that was coming off the new car ferry that I had seen arriving; the traffic lights at the main road had not yet caught up with the increased traffic numbers. The huge craft towered above the port ahead, more like the Star Ship Enterprise than a boat, umbilicals of walkways and service-ways connecting it to the land. I passed the Royal Irish Yacht Club with its colonnade of eight Ionic columns, a building once significant in size and now beginning to be lost in the scale of the modern port. The airport-like new terminus of glass and limestone seemed to grow out of a great polished granite wall, in keeping with, yet contrasting with, the original pilastered, corbelled and pedimented railway station wall across the way.

I crossed a broad paved square to reach Queen's Road, on the corner of which a wondrous piece of Victoriana survives, just a little lost amid the traffic lights, lamp standards and a multitude of signs. It is easy to miss this little gem, a cast-iron fountain with four Greek gods supporting the bowl, and herons and swans decorating the top; it was in urgent need of refurbishment, and I hoped it would not be forgotten in the midst of all Dun Laoghaire's progress. Another reminder of the Victorian era that can be passed unnoticed along the pier road are the quaint, timber-built blue-and-white shelters on the landward side of the road, complete with seating, from where holidaymakers can look out over the sea in comfort on a rainy day. There are four of these quaint relics further on; they are not used much these days owing, I suppose, to the heavy traffic on the road. Older residents of Dun Laoghaire tell me that in the 1930s and '40s they gave much appreciated shelter at night to courting couples.

It was pleasant to be out of the sun, walking along the tree-shaded pavement overlooking the harbour. Almost hidden in the foliage is the tall obelisk erected to commemorate the departure of George IV in 1821. During a craze for blowing up statues of an imperial nature in the 1950s, zealous nationalists attempted to destroy the obelisk, but only succeeded in blasting away one of the four granite balls that support it. For nearly forty years a wooden cube assisted the other three balls in their work, until, in the early 1990s, a replacement ball was installed, restoring the monument to its former dignity.

Dun Laoghaire Harbour is very much an amenity and pleasure port today: I gave up trying to count the ranks of expensive yachts and cruisers at their moorings, protected by the two great piers. Weekend sailors stood proudly on deck, sporting themselves in colourful sailing gear as they conned their yachts out through the harbour opening, while a gathering of not-so-well-off landlubbers stood under the lighthouse and looked on with mingled pleasure and a little envy. Roller bladers scooted effortlessly along the broad pier, while mothers and young children sat patiently as the dads fished, mostly unsuccessfully, from the edge of the pier. The East Pier is a most popular promenading place, believed by the many who walk it to be one mile long, providing a two-mile round trip to the lighthouse at the end and back. I have been told by a friend in the medical profession that the place is very popular with post-operative heart bypass patients, who are encouraged to walk this distance every day! It is in fact less than one-and-a-half miles out and back; I wonder what effect this is having on recovery statistics?

Across the railway line from the West Pier entrance is a little park called Moran Park, where in summer-time bowls are played on a billiard-table lawn. As an architectural student I worked on the little bowling club pavilion here, and since there was quite a lot of fun sculpture in the park, it was thought appropriate to have a new piece associated with the pavilion. A wonderful life-sized cormorant was chosen, wings outstretched to dry, made in copper by sculptor Imogen Stuart. I remember spending a sunny afternoon looking at where it might be sited to best advantage, and after much discussion with the sculptor and the contractor, it was decided to place it on the timber handrail of a balcony that cantilevered over a duck pond. It was an ideal and entirely natural position for the piece, and the sun's reflection off the pond gave the bird a shimmering appearance. Considerable thought and industry went into how the piece was to be fixed and anchored down to the structure, for safety reasons as well as security, but even so, the morning after the day it had been mounted, the bird was found to have flown, and sadly was never seen again!

On the high ground behind Moran Park stands the Royal

Marine Hotel. Little now remains of this building's high Victorian grandeur; when built in the 1860s it was a great 'pile', its roof trimmed with a glorious row of mansard windows, and its main entrance topped by an ornate tower. Further along, one of the Victorian buildings overlooking the harbour is called the Hotel Pierre; my mother enjoyed pointing it out on visits to Dun Laoghaire, because when she stayed there awaiting the ferry to Wales on her honeymoon in 1938 it was called by the less assuming name 'The Pier Hotel'.

East of the pier I walked along a rock-garden of paths and swimming places, unfortunately scattered with aluminium cans and daubed with unsightly graffiti. I had to ascend to the road to pass by the old Dun Laoghaire Baths, still going strong and echoing with the delighted screams and shouts of children. A cluster of laughing schoolgirls, probably Leaving Certificate students, sat on the whitewashed seats outside the baths attempting, not too successfully, to study. Why is it that the important examinations always seem to take place in summertime when it's so good to be young and carefree?

Sandycove

Ahead now, stretching out into the turquoise waters of rocky Scotsman's Bay and reflecting the bright sun, was Sandycove promontory, my goal for the day. I dropped down to a pathway close to the shore and stopped to watch the cormorants preening themselves atop the offshore rocks, or like Imogen Stuart's copper piece, hanging their wings out to dry. The rising tide was insinuating itself almost imperceptibly between the seaweed-draped rocks, and the smaller ones seemed to sink beneath the water, leaving for a few seconds a series of rings as if a stone had been thrown in.

Sandycove beach was alive with children, dashing back and forth and in and out of the water. The noise of screeching and laughing, echoing off the rocky sides of the cove, was deafening. A recently posted cardboard sign fixed to the low wall at the back of the cove announced:

Warning!
Beware of sudden large waves
due to arrival of new Car Ferry:
Persons should stay well back from water's edge during
ferries approach and for twenty minutes
after it's [*sic*] arrival.'

Under it was another poster, hastily put together, stating:

The New Ferry has made it very dangerous
to swim here or at the Forty Foot.
Contact local politicians to protest.
Signed
Environmental Group.

I could see there was going to be trouble ahead for the new HSS monster car ferry, dubbed locally 'Hope it Sails Soon'!

I made my way quickly past the little beach to reach the Forty Foot, a bathing place which up to recent times was an all-male preserve, well-known to hardy types who swim all year round, and those who prefer to swim naked. There are various theories as to how this granite promontory, shelving sheer and deep into the Irish Sea, got its name; some say it refers to the depth of the water here, while others say it comes from the Fortieth Foot Regiment which was stationed in the fort that stood nearby up to late in the nineteenth century. In Dublin, however, the name was once synonymous with male exclusiveness, since it was a 'men only' swimming place. After a series of protests which started in the 1970s, it was one of the last bastions to fall to political correctness, and now anyone can swim here.

At a little kiosk supervised by an elderly man I dropped a donation into a tin biscuit box. Then I walked out on to the rocky promontory and sat down in the sun. A strange mixture of people was gathered about the place, which was divided into two distinct areas by a vertical outcrop of granite and a small concrete wall. On the west side three men were sitting or lying on towels, sunning themselves in the nude. Another man, small and middle-aged, was wandering around naked, scratching his genitals now and then in an exaggerated way. Nearby were some young boys, aged about ten or eleven, undressing with voluminous towels, giggling and trick-acting, and obviously making comments about the naked men. A group of girls in their early teens, exercising their right to be there, were sitting in their modest but tight swimsuits a little further off, whispering conspiratorially, their pink faces full of the enjoyment of this risqué ambience. A couple sat high up on the rock, holding hands and gazing into each other's eyes, in a world of their own. A number of unattached middle-aged males hovered in different positions in a way that suggested they were vaguely waiting or looking for something.

A pair of young teenagers, pale-skinned in long swimming trunks, stood at the edge of the water, being egged on by a third who had already dived in. The bigger one suddenly gave the other a push and he disappeared under the water with a great splash. He surfaced immediately, shaking the water out of his hair and shouting obscenities at his attacker. He swam to the side and, leaping ashore, chased his ducker off around the corner with a continuing tirade of expletives. I had swum at the Forty Foot only once, many years before in late autumn, and it had been a very different place then. I now found it just a little sleazy, with many more agendas in the air than a refreshing swim in the company of men. I must admit to having the feeling that the Forty Foot is one of those places that has lost rather than gained from being open to everyone. Feeling vaguely uncomfortable about being there on my own, I left and walked up to the nearby Martello tower, opened in 1962 as the James Joyce Museum.

I went in through glazed doors to the reception area and, paying two pounds for my ticket, wandered upstairs. A sign on the wall warned me not to touch anything because I could be seen on the security camera. Various pieces of Joycean memorabilia and ephemera were on display, including letters and first editions, his cane, his cigar case, and his Spanish guitar, a ladies' model. I made my way up a narrow staircase to the upper room, furnished with a bed and a hammock, an iron stove, and a table with two bottles of stout and a book on it, as it is supposed to have been when James Joyce stayed here with Oliver St John Gogarty, in 1904.

Joyce was born in the Dublin suburb of Rathgar, but before he was twenty-one, apart from his boarding-school days in Clongowes Wood, he had moved home with his family on eleven different occasions, to Rathmines, Bray, Blackrock, Hardwicke Street, Fitzgibbon Street, Drumcondra, North Richmond Street, Fairview and the North Circular Road. There is little doubt that the remarkable itinerant habits of the Joyce family have provided material for many learned theses on the author and his writings.

There seem to be some differences of opinion about how long Joyce's sojourn in the Sandycove tower lasted. Gogarty wrote afterwards that he had furnished the place and that Joyce had paid the eight pounds per year rent from some money he had won in a literary competition, and that they had lived there for two years. The version which seems to be more accepted, however, is that Gogarty was living there in September 1904 with a friend when Joyce came to stay. His sojourn at the tower in Sandycove lasted, maybe characteristically, only six nights, with Joyce leaving abruptly and unnerved early one morning after Gogarty's friend had had a wild nightmare about a black panther, during which he had started shooting a revolver into the fireplace. Later that day Joyce sent a note to a friend asking him to have his belongings collected from the tower, and he never returned. Whatever length his stay was, sharp memories of tiny details of the happenings there remained with him for years after and were used in the opening section of *Ulysses.*

> They halted while Haines surveyed the tower and said at last:
> — Rather bleak in wintertime, I should say. Martello you call it?
> — Billy Pitt had them built, Buck Mulligan said, when the French were on the sea. But ours is the omphalos.

From the Joyce Tower

I climbed out on to the roof of the omphalos which, because of the strategic purpose of the building, has a marvellous all-round view of the coast; the rails for the gun that was once mounted here to defend the coast were still there, together with a little brick oven that was used to heat up the cannon-balls. I could retrace my steps by eye back over much of my journey along the coast from Howth, and could see what lay ahead for the next mile.

I left the Joyce Museum, having to make my way through a large crowd of Japanese visitors, hung down with cameras and eager to enter the place. They brought to mind an anecdote told by David Norris, the Joycean scholar. He related how he and a few friends were ensconced in a typical Dublin pub celebrating Bloomsday, when another friend burst in excitedly to announce to all that he had just heard that *Finnegans Wake* was to be translated into Japanese. An old codger at the bar turned to his friend and loudly asked, 'Our a wha?'

I walked back past Sandycove Beach, and finding a shady spot beneath a tree overlooking Scotsman's Bay, sat down to enjoy what was left of the afternoon.

9

Sandycove to Shanganagh

The following morning I was back again at Sandycove to begin the last stretch of my walk. It turned out, eventually, to be the second-last stretch, but more about that later. Joining me at Sandycove was Jonathan Williams, a literary agent who has been a good and encouraging friend since he edited my book on the Waterford coast a few years ago. I was glad to have him along, because he has lived in Sandycove for a number of years and knows the area well.

The weather had taken a turn for the worse overnight. Following two days of sunshine, the glass had plummeted, and a cold, rain-bearing front was crossing the country. The turquoise sea of the previous day was gone, and in its place a dark and brooding slate grey mass rolled offshore, occasionally tossing up out of the swell a spume-topped wave to burst thunderously against the rocks.

We had hardly set out when being in Jonathan's company began to pay off; we met and he introduced me to James Howley, author of a fine book, *The Follies and Garden Buildings of Ireland*. I congratulated him on his achievement; his book is an excellent production, a scholarly work which is at the same time a most enjoyable read.

In spite of the weather, a few hardy masochists were enjoying the cold water of the Forty Foot. We were passing by when we met another Sandycove local. A man dressed in a bathrobe emerged from the entrance to the bathing place; from his ruddy, healthy complexion it was clear he had been swimming in the scrotum-tightening Irish Sea. Spotting Jonathan, he called hallo with a jeer about Wales's lack of prowess on the rugby pitch the day before. Jonathan laughed and introduced me to Micheal Johnston.

'He's another author,' Jonathan told me; 'he has just written a book called *The Irish Senior Rowing Championship*.'

After some further rugby banter, Micheal, a son of the playwright Denis Johnston, and brother of the novelist Jennifer Johnston, went on home to get dry, and we continued on our way. Waves of misty rain swept over us as we walked up past the Joyce Tower, beyond which we had to turn inland, because in an earlier recce I had found that although the shore was passable beyond Sandycove Point, at Bullock Harbour an unscaleable wall prevents access past the last few houses on to the harbour pier. Before long, however, the castellations of Bullock Castle came into view at the end of Breffni Road, and we reached the sea again at Bullock Harbour.

It was around about here that the character of the surroundings began to change, subtly at first but more assertively as we proceeded. The order and the formality, the regulated feel to the arrangement and planning of roads, houses, terraces, and shoreline which had existed as far as Dun Laoghaire and Sandycove seemed to begin to unravel at Bullock Harbour. Although the shore bedrock had been granite since Blackrock, after Sandycove the rock asserted itself significantly on the landscape, and particularly along the edge of the sea, in great bulbous outcrops. These changes in the character of the surroundings also coincided with the end of continuous public access to the shore. Dalkey, originally a shanty town housing the labourers who worked in Dalkey Quarry, became a middle-class suburb of Dun Laoghaire in a building boom that began in the 1830s and went on for thirty years. During this time, with a few exceptions, every available piece of land was developed, and an astonishing collection of villas of all sizes and styles spread uphill into Killiney. The higgledy-piggledly nature of the sites, reflected by the wandering streets and roads connecting them, was heavily influenced by the chaotic geology of this stretch of coast, and gives the Dalkey and Killiney areas their unique character.

There was always a small protected cove at Bullock which attracted seafarers and fisher-folk, but the first man-made pier was probably built by the Cistercians from St Mary's Abbey in Dublin, who settled there in 1346. They built a church and castle in a walled bawn and exacted tolls from every fishing boat that landed its catch in the harbour; in the mid fourteenth century the herring boat tolls netted about six hundred fish a year for the monks. The little port and the hospitality provided by the monks for travellers made it an attractive arrival place from England, and over the years luminaries such as Prince Thomas of Lancaster, son of Henry IV, Walter Cowley, Henry VIII's solicitor general, and the Earl of Sussex, Lord Deputy in 1559, arrived in Ireland via Bullock. With the suppression of the monasteries, the place gradually lost its importance, and then, with the development of Dublin port and eventually that of Kingstown, the place settled back to being a little fishing harbour. The old castle had been restored by the Carmelite Sisters, who run a very large nursing home in the adjacent buildings. The modern granite retaining wall just under the castle has been carefully designed to be in keeping with the older structure, and features animal-head gargoyles from which the rain-water pours.

We walked up Harbour Road and past Bartra Hall, a large Italianate house with broad, outstretched roof eaves. Its gardens, in which is sited yet another of Dublin Bay's Martello towers, had become a building site and were reduced to heaps of earth, in preparation for the erection of another apartment block with a sea view.

At the top of Harbour Road we passed St Patrick's Church and Dalkey National School, the latter built in 1868 to the designs of Edward Carson, father of Sir Edward Carson, the barrister and Unionist leader. The work was paid for by Charles Leslie, one of Dalkey's most prominent businessmen and benefactors, in the mid nineteenth century. In 1840 he had sold part of his extensive lands along the coast to the Loreto Sisters, who built Loreto Abbey, overlooking lawns that swept down to the sea.

We walked on into Leslie Avenue, at the end of which we came to the gates to Carraig na Greine, at one time Charles Leslie's house. Signs of general disturbance and the overgrown and uncared for condition of the grounds suggested that this was another nineteenth-century demesne that is undergoing violent change. We wandered into the grounds past a pristine granite-faced gate-lodge to reach the big house, which I was surprised to find was quite a modest place. It was built from white granite in a restrained, and even austere, design, that loosened up only in the pedimented entrance supported by two Doric columns. The windows, which once had looked out over an unsurpassed view from Howth to Dalkey Island, were crudely boarded up and a rubbish skip stood in front of the house. In the 1930s the nuns of Loreto Abbey, which stands on the adjacent site, bought the Leslie house and used it until the 1980s as part of their school. Sheltered housing was subsequently built in the grounds, and it was clear that more building was about to take place; what would happen to Carraig na Greine was unclear. It reminded me of the words of L. A. G. Strong, who had connections with Sandycove and Dalkey:

> *House sold, meadow gone*
> *And garden too, to build upon.*

We turned down Coliemore Road and passed one of my favourite groups of houses in Dalkey. An archway through a terrace of early Victorian houses leads to a little court in front of Coliemore Villas, four two-storey houses with Doric door cases with fanlights over, built about 1847. The backs of the houses overlook the sea below Carraig na Greine. Before the Cliff Castle Hotel is a house called Inniscorrig, built by Sir Dominick Corrigan in the 1850s; he was an eminent medical doctor who had rooms in Merrion Square, and somehow earned the honour of having a street in Paris, rue Corrigan, named after him.

We reached the sea again at the hotel; across a few hundred metres of angry sea, Dalkey Island stretched out, topped by yet another Martello tower. It was the sixth island I had passed on my walk from the borders of Meath, but I had not been as close to either Lambay or Ireland's Eye as this, and if the weather had not been so unsuitable, I would have taken a boat over. Dalkey Island has a long history and, like Lambay, signs have been found there of stone-age settlements. Besides the Martello tower, there are the ruins of a battery on the south end, and good remains of an early Christian church, dedicated to St Begnet. The church has the characteristic antae, that is, gable walls from which short continuations of the side walls project a little, like pilasters — a feature unique to the earlier stone churches of Ireland. The building is in reasonably good condition, in spite of being lived in for a period by the men who built the Martello tower and the battery. It was also the focus of a popular public festival that took place annually through the eighteenth century, of the election and coronation of the King of Dalkey. Great crowds, in suitable fancy dress, flocked to the island for the festivities, and there was music and dancing throughout the day. The celebrations culminated in the coronation of the mock king, which took place in the church, during which invited guests, known for their wit and eloquence, made sham speeches of congratulation. At the end of the ceremonies the crowd drank to the health of 'His facetious Majesty, King of Dalkey, Emperor of the Muglins, Prince of the Holy Island of Magee, Elector of Lambay and Ireland's Eye, Defender of his own Faith and Respecter of others, Sovereign of the Illustrious Order of the Lobster and Periwinkle'.

Dalkey Island

The little harbour below the hotel, Coliemore Harbour, with its strange trail of boatmen's sheds that seem to grow out of the granite rocks, was once an important place. Dalkey Island provides a certain amount of shelter to the land here, and when tides and winds in Dublin Bay prevented ships from gaining safe access to Dublin port, Coliemore served as an alternative embarkation point. A large granite boulder stood in a prominent place overlooking the harbour, with a hollowed-out rectangle in its surface where once a bronze plaque, listing the names of the important people who used the port, was mounted; today these prominenti are as forgotten as the harbour's former days of glory.

A very wet, misty rain came dowsing down as we passed by the harbour and started uphill, separated now from the sea by houses. On the right is a tiny cottage called Bella Vista, a name that I have seen attached to many houses where the vista was anything but bella; however, never was the name so rightly given as in this case. The view from the front windows of the cottage included Dalkey Sound and Island and the Irish Sea beyond through a frame of trees.

There is a little park across the road that I had never noticed before, and Jonathan led me into it and down by a winding path to the rocky shore again. It is called Dillon's Park, and I initially assumed that it had been called after some well-known person of that name. Not at all, I was told by a friend who lives in the area; it was named after a Mrs Dillon who kept a tea-room here in the 1930s, whom Hugh Leonard describes in his memoir *Home Before Night*: she 'was fat and had whiskers and kept the little hut of a shop at the gate where you bought fizz-bags'.

There is not much to it, this little park: it consists of a Scots pine or two, a broken-down concrete and chicken-wire sculpture of a pair of goats, and paths that wind between bulbous outcrops of granite and thick groves of veronica and gorse bushes. Its rocky shore-side location, however, overlooking the fast-flowing waters between the mainland and Dalkey Island, makes it a very special place.

I was interested to see if we could make our way around to Killiney along the shore, so we followed a narrow corridor through gorse going south along a low, rocky cliff. As I looked across the sound towards the island, a seal popped its head out of the turbulent waters below, and regarded us curiously. Jonathan had not noticed and continued along the path; I stopped and quickly unslung my camera case. The rain did not help, but in spite of it I got a picture of the seal, his head raised out of the waves, tilted to one side with a quizzical expression. It was a repeat of what had happened on my first day walking this coast, and it might even have been the same seal: I thought it nicely appropriate that I should again have such a meeting on my last day's walk.

I hurried to catch up with Jonathan, and reached him where he had stopped on a platform of rock from where there was a wonderfully misty view of grey Bray Head sweeping around into Killiney Bay, backed by the conical Sugarloaf hills and the rounded Wicklow Mountains. I could see for the first time the southern end of Killiney Beach where my odyssey would come to an end. The view was a consolation prize, however; barbed wire-topped railings blocked any further advance along the cliffs, and we had to retrace our steps.

I have been back to this little park since, and spent a wonderful early morning half-hour gazing out across the water. It must be a particularly good marine habitat here, where the waters rush in and out of the sound, because during the time I stood there I saw two more seals, many cormorants and terns, even a raven, and I could hardly believe my eyes when a dolphin arched its leisurely way southwards towards Killiney Bay.

Back on the road, we made our way under beech trees to Sorrento Terrace, a Victorian show-piece completed in 1855, and designed by William Masterson, architect for the Royal St George Yacht Club. It was originally planned as a crescent, but this arrangement was found to be unsuitable owing to the volume of bedrock that would have to be excavated at the inner ends of the block. The back windows, including those of the basement, look out on a most spectacular view over Killiney Bay.

Opposite the terrace, Jonathan took me into another little public park, a place one could easily miss, accessed by a granite gateway that could be the entrance to a house. We climbed a series of looping paths around a high outcrop of granite to its summit, where during the Emergency an anti-aircraft battery had been located. From the comfort of a little seat, a spectacular view was to be had. The truculent weather had produced some angry skies to the north over the Hill of Howth, and the sea was innumerable shades of grey-green; across Killiney Bay the Wicklow coast showed faintly beyond Bray Head. In the foreground below there was a voyeur's eye-view into all the front rooms of Sorrento Terrace!

It is nice to think that this fine coast is not just a preserve of the financially better-off; these two little parks in Dalkey allow the general public to share in the enjoyment of the beauty of the area. On the eastern side of the park, set into a thor of granite bedrock, is a ceramic plaque commemorating the Dalkey-born Elizabethan poet and musician, John Dowland. Dowland was a contemporary and friend of Shakespeare's, and it is boasted locally that he gave the bard most of his ideas!

Killiney Bay

We continued south, turning on to the Vico Road, above which a pastel composition of villas and houses, all with a wonderful outlook, clings to the steep hillside like steps of stairs. Killiney Bay has been compared to the Bay of Naples, and it must be for this reason: that many of the houses here have evocative Italian names; along the Vico Road (could it be named after the Italian philosopher and historian, Giovanni Vico?) we passed 'Capri', and climbed uphill by 'Milano' and 'La Scala'.

At the first opportunity we turned in through an opening in the wall and followed a path, bordered by banks of mallow, valerian, white bluebells and bird's-foot trefoil, down towards the cliffs. We crossed the railway line by way of a hollow-sounding metal bridge which brought us to the edge of a promontory called on my map Hawks Cliff, where a sign warned that the cliffs are unsafe and dangerous. We looked at the rough sea below and the breakers rushing on to a very rocky shore, and decided to return to the Vico Road and descend again at White Rock, further along.

The Vico Road led up gently uphill along a granite wall topped by a cordon of the healthiest veronica I have ever seen, backed by a line of holm oaks and scots pines. At a house called 'Sunnyside', its roof adorned with many strange chimneys, the road used to, until 1887, come to an end at a wall. Dalkey folk called the place 'The End of the World'. Beyond the wall was private land, the demesne of the Warren family who lived in Killiney Castle. The legacy of that former ownership is that the open land sloping steeply down to the cliffs, called the Vico Fields, was preserved from development, and is there today for the enjoyment of all.

A little beyond 'Sunnyside', Jonathan and I left the road again and descended a path through banks of yellow rape-seed, the massed flower heads hung down with rainwater, to cross the railway again and reach Killiney Strand at a place called White Rock. As we neared the beach and the thundering, hissing sound of the waves crashing on to the shingle grew louder, I became aware of another sound drifting in and out of the background, the haunting lilt of a musical instrument. It was most puzzling, almost surreal, but as we passed an old concrete shelter, the volume suddenly increased, and I saw that the plaintive sound was emanating from a clarinet being played by a lone musician, standing in the shelter and seeming to play to the sea. I suppose he was practising, and found the acoustics of the shelter suitable, but it certainly made for an eerie arrival through misting rain on to Killiney Strand.

I pointed out to Jonathan a narrow, steep and stepped passageway overhung with Virginia creeper that exited on to the beach nearby, relating how I had found some time before it passed the back door to U2 star Bono's house, a door painted in fascinating grafitti. Every square inch of the door was covered with messages, most neatly written. 'Thanks for your music, from Ingrid', 'U2 is my religion, Bono Vox is my God', 'We come from

Montreal to see you, we love you', and 'Give me one more chance and you'll be satisfied'. It was a kind of shrine, the nearest these ardent fans could get to their hero, where they lovingly wrote out their prayers and exhortations in the hope that, sneaking down one morning for a swim, his eyes might just see their message. All the notes were cloyingly adulatory, and carefully signed; I had been relieved to see, however, almost submerged in the praises, the work of a wag who wrote the plaintive message, 'Bono, I'm pregnant!'

The sand was quite firm underfoot for a while, and made a welcome change from tarmac. In spite of the poor weather, there was plenty of activity on the beach, with people walking their dogs and sea-bass fishermen tending their long sea-rods. The wind had increased and the sky behind Sorrento Terrace was dark and ominous, while the sea had a strange pale green look to it, marbled through with white horses.

The erosion of the cliffs along the southern end of the beach was considerable; I knew that the old Wicklow railway line, which used to run along the clifftop, had disappeared into the sea early in the 1900s, but I was surprised to see, by the evidence in the debris of walls and other constructions scattered on the gravel beach, that the problem was continuing.

Gravel soon took the place of the sand, and made walking a little more difficult. Killiney is a good place to learn about the great Ice Ages, as the features of the surroundings, the scenery of the place, are almost all the result of the last glaciation. The exposed bedrock on top of Killiney Hill bears the scratches, or striations, made by ice cap that covered the area up to twelve thousand years ago. Glaciers are constantly, if very slowly, on the move, and the direction of the flow of this last glacier can be clearly read from these rocks. As the one-thousand-metre thick ice sheet passed over the projecting knobs of granite, as well as grinding grooves in the surface, it rubbed the rock smooth on the side from which it was advancing, while plucking away rough blocks of rock on the 'leeward' side. Rock hummocks eroded by the ice in this way are known as *roches moutonnées*, from some fanciful idea that they can look like a flock of sheep.

The clays and rocks that make up the cliffs that line Killiney beach were deposited under this great ice sheet by rivers of melting ice, and over subsequent millennia, cut back by the sea in an action that clearly is continuing today. The cliffs tell in layers the history of these great ice-sheet rivers; stratified stones and rocks suggest periods of substantial melting of the ice, generating torrential flows, while layers of fine sands are evidence of periods of slow melting, producing an even, consistent flow. The pebbles on the beach are all that remains of the cliffs that have already been washed away by the sea, and they tell another story. Individual stones can suggest how far the ice sheet has actually travelled as it 'flowed': for instance, the Killiney gravel is composed mostly of limestone pebbles, and the nearest limestone occurring naturally is at least ten miles away. The differences in the colouring, and sizes of individual crystals of the many granite stones represented show that they have been brought together here from far and wide. There is another pebble that can easily be found on the beach which has been delivered from much further afield: a pink-purple stone, with an unusual granite composition, known only on the island of Ailsa Craig, off the Scottish coast, more than a hundred miles to the north.

It is said that on Killiney Strand Samuel Beckett's Molloy collected 'a store of sucking stones', the sucking of which 'appeases, soothes, makes you forget your hunger, forget your thirst'. Molloy's stone-sucking was apparently inspired by a Dublin character known as Stoney Pockets, who kept himself straight and erect by distributing the right amount of stones into his left and right pockets. I once knew a farm labourer who always carried a couple of sea-pebbles in his pocket for sucking from time to time, like Beckett's Molloy. This man swore that different stones had a different taste, and he had particular favourites!

At the early research stage, I had experienced some difficulty in identifying precisely where the boundary between Wicklow and Dublin lay. Originally I had assumed that it was the Dargle river, but was surprised to find that the Dargle flowed into the sea south of the actual boundary, which did not seem to follow any particular physical feature. When I was arranging walking the last stretch with Jonathan, he mentioned that friends of his lived just on the boundary; subsequently we were invited to call in when we had finished our walk, which we should do within a short distance of his house.

At what I thought, therefore, was the southern end of Shanganagh and near the county boundary, we climbed another concrete staircase up to the cliffs to reach the end of a narrow road. A railway bridge over the road was all that was left of the old Wicklow railway line, and we followed the ghost of the line along the grassy clifftop. A man came walking towards us with a dog, and I stopped and asked him if he knew where the Dublin-Wicklow border was.

'County Wicklow and County Dublin, ah, that would be', he paused and looked back where he had come from, 'somewhere between here and Bray Harbour there. Just over the brow of that hill, there, I think it is, but you see the border may not be a straight line; it may meander. Just as you come into Bray, at Old Conna, the border is there, but I think it meanders back towards this way. Where exactly it is I couldn't tell you.'

I thanked him and we walked on a little further until we reached the northern end of the Woodbrook Golf Club, where an earthen bank created not just a fence, but a mearing, a very definite physical boundary. I was certain that this was it, and Jonathan congratulated me on my arrival at the end of the journey from Dublin's border with County Meath. I was disappointed in some ways to have come to the end of my odyssey. It was a bit anti-climactic; the journey had been a fascinating experience. As we retraced our steps to find the house of Philip and Patsy Harvey, Jonathan's friends, I was also a little relieved to have reached this stage of the project, and was looking forward to beginning to write about my experiences.

It was not until months later, as I was completing the manuscript for this book, and examining detailed maps, that the truth dawned; I had not reached County Wicklow at all! The true boundary was nearly a mile further south from where I had turned back, contented that I had finished the journey. Now this was a bit of a puzzle, because the boundary indicated on the map was very close indeed to the Dargle river, and I wondered why a county boundary would ignore such a significant physical feature? Long-established land boundaries, particularly major ones, tend to coincide with physical features, such as established and dependable watercourses, because these were convenient lines for neighbours to agree upon. Certainly our ancient townlands, land divisions unique to Ireland, used watercourses where possible. I was curious why this important county boundary would ignore an adjacent physical feature, and so I rang the Geography Department of Trinity College, Dublin to see if they could shed any light on the subject. Dr Michael Quigley came to my aid, and within an hour of my phone call rang back with a possible explanation. The 'shiring' or subdivision of Wicklow, Carlow and Wexford into counties did not take place until about 1610. The town of Bray, however, an early Norman stronghold on the edge of the O'Tooles' and O'Byrnes' territories, had been in existence since at least the early thirteenth century when King John granted an annual fair there. It is possible that the lands claimed by the town of Bray simply did not stop at the Dargle, and when the new shire boundaries were being struck for Wicklow, the old boundary, which seems to deliberately avoid the Dargle and wander about before finally terminating at the seashore, was respected.

So, months later, I found myself back on the shore at the end of Quinn's Road in Shanganagh, where my southern progress had come to a premature conclusion. An elderly man in a gabardine coat and a tweed cap sat at the bottom of the steps, gazing out to sea. I asked him if he knew where the boundary of Wicklow was.

'It's down there, around the corner,' he said. 'I think there's a sign on it; there's a kind of stream running into the sea at the place where the boundary is. It's easy to get to at low tide.'

We chatted for a while and he told me that he had recently returned to Shanganagh after thirty-eight years working in England. Down here by the sea reminded him of his boyhood, except that he had been very surprised to observe the extent of the erosion that had taken place over those years. The old railway line had disappeared, and the newer one looked as if it would go soon. I asked him when the 'newer one' had been built.

'It's very sad that. It was summer-time when the work on the new railway line was finished, and there was no work to be had in Ireland. The day they were left go, most of the men slung their belongings on their backs and walked to Kingstown for the ferry to England. Within a week they were in the British Army, the only work available there. It was the month of June 1914, and within a few months they had all been killed in France.'

With this haunting tale echoing in my ears, I set out along the gravel beach. It was a bright, breezy day after about three weeks of storms. The sea was still agitated and sent in a constant array of breakers to crash on the shore. A line of substantially eroded and precarious cliffs stretched in a series of promontories towards the distant humpback of Bray Head. A sign standing crooked in the shingle of the beach said 'Beware of the Cliffs', and it was very obvious that another layer of land could at any moment collapse, and await the incoming tide to wash the clays away and add a new collection of multicoloured pebbles to the beach.

In one place a sandy layer at the top of the cliff was perforated with many little holes. I recognised them as the nest tunnels of the sandmartin, each of which would be over a metre deep. These tiny birds fly in great flocks from Africa to spend the summer and give birth to their young in northern Europe; when they are in residence it is a pleasure to watch them sporting and playing along the cliffs.

Bray Head

Along the shore, twenty metres from the base of the cliffs, were what looked at a distance like outcrops of rock, but on closer examination they turned out to be lengths of the once massive stone wall that retained the Victorian rail embankment. The twenty metres from the cliff represented the amount of erosion that has taken place since the embankment began to be washed away in the early 1900s. Signs of recent falls included a series of concrete fence-posts suspended from the cliff like a giant necklace. In one place an enormous granite boulder projected precariously out of the boulder clay half-way up, and I wondered when it would come crashing down. A moulting grey-backed crow coasted along the edge of the clifftop like some shredded black kite and passed overhead, curiously watching my movements.

As I neared Bray, the height of the cliffs began to reduce, and the nature of the shingle underfoot began to change. More and more rounded fragments of terracotta brick could be identified among the pebbles, and increasing amounts of green and brown glass glinted through stone-worn opaqueness, and shards of blue delph. Inevitably, at the top of the beach, the collection of plastic bottles and bags began to increase also.

Soon the cliffs dipped to receive a declivity, a narrow ravine which looked as if one time a stream had flowed on to the beach here. There was no sign apparent as the man at Shanganagh had suggested, but there was a pair of poles which could have held a sign. I walked up along the stream bed through a copse of elder scrub and creepers and found that I was at the southern boundary of the Woodbrook Golf Club.

It looked as if it might be the county boundary, but I did not want to be fooled again, so I decided to carry on to Bray pier, which looked to be a few hundred metres away. Beyond the pier I knew I would find the Dargle, and without a doubt I would then be in County Wicklow.

Within fifty metres I came to where a strong and swiftly flowing stream was pouring out across the beach. It flowed to one side of two ruined granite buttresses that projected out on to the beach, no doubt marking where the old railway line had once bridged the stream. This looked more like a boundary! I continued on and mounted the breakwater which took me on to Bray Harbour. The tide was out and a woman was feeding eighteen swans and a host of seagulls on the seaweed-covered sands. I crossed the bridge over the Dargle to make certain of the completion of my coastal journey, and made my way to the Harbour Bar to celebrate the moment.

As I walked, I looked south to where Bray Head reached into the Irish Sea and, entering the warm atmosphere of the pub, began to wonder how long it would take me to walk the coast of County Wicklow.

Select Bibliography

Bates, Peadar, *Portrane and Donabate*, 1988

Bence Jones, Mark, *The Twilight of the Ascendancy*, 1987

Berghaus, Erwin, *The History of Railways*, 1964

Bourke, Edward, *Shipwrecks of the Irish Coast*, 1994

Caprani, Vincent, *A View from the DART*, 1986

Cosgrave, Dillon, *North Dublin*, 1977

Cullen, L. M., *Princes and Pirates: The Dublin of 1783–1983*, 1983

de Courcy, J.W., *The Liffey in Dublin*, 1996

Flynn, Arthur, *Ringsend and her Sister Villages*, 1990

Gilligan, H.A., *A History of the Port of Dublin*, 1988

Healy, E., C. Moriarty and G. O'Flaherty, *The Book of the Liffey*, 1988

Hurley, Michael J., *Baldoyle, A View from the Grandstand*, 1989

Igoe, Vivien, *A Literary Guide to Dublin*, 1994

Joyce, Weston St John, *The Neighbourhood of Dublin*, 1912

Keane, C. Campbell and B. Brady (editors), *Working Life in Fingal 1936–1959*, 1994

Lalor, Brian, *Dublin Bay from Killiney to Howth*, 1989

Latham, Harry, *St Patrick's Church of Ireland Dalkey*, 1992

A Select Bibliography

Lewis, Samuel, *A Topographical Dictionary of Ireland*, 1837

Long, Bill, *Bright Light, White Water*, 1993

Mitchell, Frank, *Shell Guide to Reading the Irish Countryside*, 1987

O'Connell, Michael, *Fingal* n.d.

O'Dwyer, Frederick, *Lost Dublin*, 1981

Pearson, Peter, *Dun Laoghaire Kingstown*, 1981

Rothery, Seán, *Ireland and the New Architecture*, 1991

The British Association Handbook to the Dublin District, 1908

The Dublin Penny Journal, 1830–34

The Tourist Illustrated Handbook for Ireland 1853

Index

Index